Quarterly Essay

CONTENTS

I0038945

Quarterly Essay is published four times a year by Black Inc., an imprint of Schwartz Media Pty Ltd. Publisher: Morry Schwartz.

ISBN 978-1-86395-526-3 ISSN 1832-0953

Subscriptions – 1 year (4 issues): $49 within Australia incl. GST. Outside Australia $79. 2 years (8 issues): $95 within Australia incl. GST. Outside Australia $155.

Payment may be made by Mastercard or Visa, or by cheque made out to Schwartz Media. Payment includes postage and handling.

To subscribe, fill out and post the subscription card or form inside this issue, or subscribe online:

www.quarterlyessay.com
subscribe@blackincbooks.com
Phone: 61 3 9486 0288

Correspondence should be addressed to:

The Editor, Quarterly Essay
37–39 Langridge Street
Collingwood VIC 3066 Australia
Phone: 61 3 9486 0288 / Fax: 61 3 9486 0244
Email: quarterlyessay@blackincbooks.com

Editor: Chris Feik. Management: Sophy Williams, Caitlin Yates. Publicity: Elisabeth Young. Design: Guy Mirabella. Assistant Editor/Production Coordinator: Nikola Lusk. Typesetting: Duncan Blachford.

FAIR SHARE

Country and City
in Australia

Judith Brett

"We live in a big country and should all share the cost."—Bruce Evans, ABC Country
Viewpoint, 11 February 2002

In the days after the 2010 election, as both Julia Gillard and Tony Abbott
courted the votes of the independents in the hope of winning the crucial
one or two seats that would deliver them government, the voice of the
Australian country re-asserted itself. Three of the four independents were
from rural Australia: Tony Windsor, who has held the seat of New England
in New South Wales since 2001; Bob Katter, member for the huge, far
north Queensland seat of Kennedy since 1993; and Rob Oakeshott, who
first won the NSW coastal seat of Lyne at a by-election in 2008. All had
once been members of the National Party.

The styles were different: Tony Windsor in his short-sleeved, open-
necked shirt was thoughtful and courteous; Bob Katter aggressively
flamboyant with his wide-brimmed Stetson worn indoors and out; and
Rob Oakeshott didn't know when to stop talking. But they all articulated
arguments and claims which had a long history in Australian political

life and had been scarcely heard in an election campaign centred on the marginal seats of the capital cities.

In August last year, as we waited to see whether Labor or the Coalition would form the government, Tony Windsor and Bob Katter talked to Leigh Sales on the ABC's *Lateline*. Rob Oakeshott couldn't join the conversation because of the poor state of telecommunications outside the capital cities. Sales asked her guests about the population debate.

> *Tony Windsor:* It's been a debate that's been politically marketed into Western Sydney because that's where both of them think that the balance of power will be actually determined, the winner will be determined in those western suburbs. And that's a nonsense to have that debate when there's massive regional areas that haven't been developed, could be developed … there's unused infrastructure in many of these communities and the population could expand and grow in some of these areas, but not in Sydney anymore. We've done too much of that. But government policy has driven that.
>
> The centralist policies that we've had in the past have all been about driving people into a feedlot, and that feedlot's Sydney and suddenly the feedlot is full. And now we're talking about closing down the rest of Australia because we can't fit any more people in the feedlot.
>
> *Bob Katter:* We don't want them to go to the cities. We want to take some of the people out of Sydney and Melbourne and put them where they can have a civilised lifestyle, which we can provide for them in Australia … if you drop a series of hydrogen bombs from the back of Cairns, the other side of Mareeba, 30 kilometres from Cairns, all the way across to Broome, you won't kill anybody. There's nobody living there … there's about 95 per cent of the surface area of Australia – just cut out the little coastal strip and a little dot around Perth: the population's not much different than when Captain Cook arrived. There's only 670,000 people living on

95 per cent of the surface area of the country. And, I mean, we're talking about overpopulation! ... Everyone is just moving away from rural Australia, where we've got miles of infrastructure that's not being used, and cramming into the cities. I mean, and there's not the slightest word in all of this election campaign about that problem or repopulating the people into these demographic centres where we can absorb huge amounts of population.

Not only do both men believe in a big Australia and the need to fill the empty land; both also reveal deep-seated assumptions that country life is better. Katter is frank: get people out of Sydney and Melbourne to where they can have a civilised life; Windsor's image of the city as a feedlot is rich with unsavoury associations of passivity, overcrowding and the smell of shit.

The country and the city are cultural as well as geographic locations. The brilliant cultural critic Raymond Williams has described the long history of the rivalry between the Country and the City in Western thought. Since the Romans, clusters of moral and cultural meanings have formed round these complex words and there have been continuing arguments about which is the best place for people to live: the country with its sturdy independence, nearness to nature and friendly people; or the sophisticated city with its cultural richness and the freedom of anonymity. That's the upside. But each also has a downside: the city as overcrowded, dirty, full of sin and temptation, a place of alienation and lonely people; the countryside as backward and oppressively conservative, peopled by hayseeds and rural idiots. And so on. The interplay of the virtues and vices of the country and the city is different in different times and places. Sometimes the country will have the upper hand, sometimes the city. But always there will be grievances, as claims about respective virtues and vices are marshalled in political struggles over the allocation of symbolic and material resources.

Since at least the 1970s in Australia the city has had the upper hand and the country has been pushed aside. In fact, by the beginning of the twenty-first century, the word "country" had all but disappeared from Australia's political vocabulary as a word for the settled countryside, replaced by "regional" for major non-metropolitan centres and "rural" for areas of sparse population, although regional often does for both. Even country Australia's very own political party has abandoned the word: in 1982 the Australian Country Party changed its name to the National Party of Australia in a vain attempt to turn itself from a sectional party of farmers and rural small business into a broad-based conservative party. It is only in country music that the word is common, and even there it is shadowed by the Aboriginal meaning of country to evoke spiritual belonging to one's traditional land.

It wasn't always thus. Once the country believed itself to be the true face of Australia: sunburnt men and capable women raising crops and children, enduring isolation, hardship and a fickle environment, carrying the nation on their sturdy backs. There were reasons for this, as this essay will show. For almost 200 years after white settlement began, city Australia needed the country: to feed it, to earn its export income, to fill the empty land, to provide it with distinctive images of the nation being built in the great south land. This gave the country strong claims for resources and it pushed them hard. In August last year, with the fate of the government again in the hands of country Australians, we heard these claims again, and so too the grievance that the contribution and potential of the country were easily forgotten by politicians chasing city votes.

As Katter told Leigh Sales:

> the position of rural Australia will be taken into consideration, which has not been the case over the last twelve years under the LNP and over the last three years under the ALP and the ALP previous to that. We were just not taken into consideration at all. The party system has served the big city interests, the big corporate interests, but it has not served the interests of ordinary people, 30 per cent of us, which live outside of the major capital cities.

Windsor hoped a hung parliament "might be a wake-up call for the parties that running these Western Sydney-type campaigns leaves a lot of people out of the debate and country people are sick of being left out."

After seventeen tense days of negotiation and speculation, the three country independents announced their decisions: Katter would back the Opposition and Windsor and Oakeshott would support the previous government. Reportedly, Windsor and Oakeshott sat down in Windsor's office with an A4 sheet of paper divided into two columns, one headed Labor and the other Coalition. They lined up the generous offers each side had made of support for the regions. The clincher was Labor's commitment to broadband, described by Windsor as the most important piece of infrastructure for rural Australia.

Labor drew up a post-election agreement with Windsor and Oakeshott, which contained an appendix titled "Commitment to Regional Australia". It began with a preamble that justified the special treatment the agreement promised:

> One out of every three Australians lives in a community that is part of regional Australia. These are the Australians who are chiefly responsible for the fresh food that every day is on the table of Australian families in cities, suburbs and across the nation.
>
> They are the Australians who generate wealth from our natural resources, who play a leading role in sectors like tourism and manufacturing, and who often battle the adversities of drought, floods, fire and cyclones.
>
> They may choose to live in regional communities because of the lifestyle and the benefits to family life that it offers. Their labours drive our nation's prosperity, particularly through the small businesses they run, but too often they have not been given their fair share of Australia's successes.
>
> The quality of healthcare, education, broadband, transport and infrastructure has been allowed to fall behind that of other parts of

the nation, leading to continued urbanisation and discontent in regional areas.

There followed a promised cornucopia of government-delivered services and benefits. Country Australia was to be given its own cabinet-level minister, a new dedicated department, a cabinet sub-committee, a new House of Representatives committee, a coordinating unit in the Department of Prime Minister and Cabinet, and a Regional Development Policy Centre. Spending on the country was to be made more transparent in budget reporting at all levels, and there was to be lots of it: a National Broadband Network, investment in regional health, education, infrastructure, agriculture and water management.

The undertaking was that regional Australia will get its "fair share." The term "fair share" is used three times in the "Commitment", along with "fair hearing," "fair return," "equitable" distribution of funds, and commitment to "the equity principle" in the formulae governments use to distribute funds. In the case of broadband, "fair and equal access" was to be achieved by government putting in place a subsidy to create a uniform wholesale price so that regional users can pay the same prices as people in the city. In a big country, this is a very expensive commitment! Sometimes regional Australia was to have priority; for example, it was to be "the first to receive funding under key education initiatives and reforms." Why? Presumably because it had fallen so far behind, though no evidence was provided to support this. Or did the idea of a "fair share" speak for itself?

"Fair share" is a companion term in the Australian political lexicon to the more familiar "fair go," the shorthand used to sum up Australia's historic egalitarian ethos. "Fair share" is not quite so common in everyday speech, but it evokes the same tradition and its reliance on the umpire of the state to settle competing claims.

According to the historian John Hirst, "fair go" is an Australian invention, deriving from the English "fair play," and it means keeping to the rules, treating people equally and giving someone a decent chance. It was a cardinal principle of the labour movement and its struggle for fair and decent wages and state assistance to individuals through the benefits of the welfare state. More recently John Howard also evoked it in his projection of himself as an ordinary Australian bloke who believed that, along with practical mateship, the fair go was one of the "uniquely Australian concepts" which underpinned our society. He linked it firmly to individual wellbeing and basic welfare entitlements.

What of "fair share"? Most often when Australians think about their country's egalitarian traditions, they think of the informality of manners and absence of relations of deference – such as sitting in the front of taxis and an aversion to tipping – and of conditions in the workplace – high minimum wages and reasonable working conditions. They think, that is, about class relations. But there is another historically important strand of Australian egalitarianism that is focused on regional or spatial equity. Since federation, part of the Australian commitment to fairness has been a commitment to regional equality, to keeping living standards relatively equal across the continent so that Australia would not have very poor and very rich regions, such as the sort of differences which have long held between the north and south of Italy. The Tasmanian premier, Lara Giddings, appeals to this idea as she fights off accusations from other premiers that Tasmania has become a mendicant, bludging off the more productive and better managed states: "It's all about Aussie mateship and a fair go. I have great faith in the values of equity and fairness in Australia … We are a regional economy and we will not survive without the bigger states helping to cross-subsidise our regional economy." Built into the notion of what it is to be an Australian is an idea of certain social entitlements, shared access to basic services, a shared minimum standard of living wherever one lives, whether in a poor state like Tasmania, a small country town or the remote outback.

Of course, this has not always been achieved, but it has been an aim, an ideal, part of what it means to be an Australian which can be invoked by groups arguing for their just deserts. Appeals to fairness imply the presence of an adjudicator, a person or an institution to decide what is fair and to implement it. And for Australians this has been the government. Country people might have been fiercely anti-labour and opposed to the socialism of the union movement, but when it came to the belief that the government's main responsibility was to provide the resources necessary to sustain individual and collective life in the country, they were as socialist as anyone. "Country Party socialism," it was called. Although at political odds over the role of unionised labour, workers and country people were united in the belief that the state should ensure that they all received their fair share of the country's wealth.

Two months after the independents made their call, rural problems were again centre-stage, with angry farmers in Griffith and Deniliquin burning copies of the Murray-Darling Basin Authority's draft plan to restore environmental flows to the sprawling inland river system. Scientists argue that the ecosystem is on the point of collapse. In 2009, Australia had watched as water levels in the Coorong dropped so low that wetlands at the Murray's mouth risked permanent acidification; Adelaide's water was barely drinkable. The draft plan recommended that to maintain the health of key environmental features, much less water be diverted for other purposes, irrigation in particular. Mayhem followed the plan's release, with angry irrigators shouting abuse at the authority's representatives, who vainly tried to explain the reasons for the huge cuts to water allocations. Reductions of up to 45 per cent were recommended across the system. How could towns such as Griffith or Mildura, towns built on irrigation, possibly survive? What would become of the Riverina? And who would feed the cities? "It's going to take a lot of Bush-Tucker to feed Melbourne and Sydney," read a placard in Deniliquin. The Nationals' state member for Murrumbidgee, Adrian Piccoli, said the plan was devastating for his community. "You just can't sit in Canberra, make these kinds of decisions with people's lives and expect there to be no response and expect people even to be calm about it. People have invested their lives in their businesses and to see them threatened in this way, of course people are angry."

The government, surprised by the strength of the protest and the visceral anger, wobbled, with much talk of the need to get the balance right, and promised more research on the social and economic impact of the cuts. Had it really thought the irrigators would just roll over? In December, Mike Taylor, the chair of the authority, resigned over the government's downgrading of the priority of environmental concerns.

Rural protests are a recurring feature of Australian politics, with farmers and townsfolk rallying against city interests and city-based politics. In the early part of the twentieth century the focus was on taxation and government spending, and sometimes on trade policy. Why should country people's taxes be spent on city infrastructure? Why should country people pay tariffs on goods to subsidise the wages of unionised workers? Robert Menzies' father, James Menzies, a storekeeper in the new Wimmera town of Jeparit, was a member of the short-lived Kyabram League, formed shortly after federation to protest against the increased taxation which would come with the new level of government and the reduced number of state parliamentarians to make way for the federal chaps. Contemporary rural protests are mainly about environmental policies: the mountain cattlemen riding up Bourke Street in their Akubras and Driza-Bones to protest against the Victorian government's ending of grazing leases in alpine national parks; timber workers blockading Canberra in the 1980s over forestry agreements; irrigators burning the Murray-Darling draft plan. The enemies are scientists, city environmentalists and politicians pandering to the green inner-city vote. For a brief few years in the late 1990s rural protest was drawn to Pauline Hanson's One Nation Party, though that party cast its net wider than the disaffected rural vote, to disaffected older Anglo-Australians more generally.

City reactions to these sporadic eruptions of rural anger range from sympathy through to indifference, bemusement, condescension and contemptuous dismissal. The stock figure of the whinging farmer makes regular appearances, often with reference to the unshakable pessimism of poet John O'Brien's farmer Hanrahan. "We'll all be rooned," said Hanrahan, "Before the year is out." No matter how good the season, Hanrahan sees ruin just round the corner – though this year, as the drought has been broken by devastating floods, such pessimism seems vindicated. The media coverage of Pauline Hanson and her supporters drew on the same images of rural idiocy and redneck prejudice that are regularly on show in city commentary on country music, as line dancers and wailing singers in fringed shirts are held up for the amusement of urban sophisticates. Class prejudice is at play here as well, interacting with rurality to further distance the country from the city. Bob Katter, with his swaggering walk and large Texan hat, plays defiantly to this cultural divide as he tries to focus the political mind on the realities of life for many outside the nation's cities:

> I'd just say to you that I've watched friends of mine commit suicide. I've watched hundreds of my close friends bankrupted and their lives destroyed. I've watched towns literally close down before my eyes. I've watched football teams cease to exist. I've watched all of those things happen for 25 years and I'm not saying it's payback time now, but I'm asking for a fairer go and I'm entitled to do that.

Watching the events of the second half of last year with a historian's eye, I was struck by another continuity in the rural protests: location. Katter, Windsor and Oakeshott are all from areas with strong traditions of political autonomy, which had once aspired to separate statehood; so too the angry Riverina farmers. In the 1880s North Queensland proposed a new colony north of the Tropic of Capricorn with Townsville as its capital. North Queensland is half a continent away from Brisbane and there was growing resentment of the capital's dominance.

In the 1920s and 1930s two areas of New South Wales attempted to shrug off the control of Sydney and form new states: one in New England and one in the Riverina. Oakeshott's and Windsor's electorates are both within the boundaries of the proposed new state of New England. It is easy to forget how historically contingent Australia's state boundaries are. Northern New South Wales is much closer to Brisbane than to Sydney. When Queensland separated from New South Wales in 1859, many of the inhabitants of the Tweed, Richmond and Clarence districts, as well as the New England tablelands, wanted to be part of the new colony. Sydney was a distant centre of power and viewed with suspicion, much as Canberra now is, and when hostility to Sydney was aroused, so too was the desire for separation. Why was the NSW government spending huge amounts of money building the Sydney Harbour Bridge and the underground when there was no bridge across the Clarence River at Grafton and its mouth was unnavigable? The New Staters believed in decentralisation, or development for the regions, and resented the "Sydney octopus" strangling their potential for growth.

Now barely remembered in national history, the New State movements were widespread and vigorous. A convention in Armidale in 1921 attracted 220 delegates from 124 New State leagues across 116 northern towns. When the Country Party entered a coalition government in 1922, the movement waned, but it sprung back to life in the Depression to fight Jack Lang, the radical premier of New South Wales. Lang gave New Staters a new, urgent reason for separation; they did not want to be dragged into the ignominy of his proposed debt repudiation. In 1931 "monster rallies" of 10,000 people were held in Wagga Wagga on the banks of the Murrumbidgee to protest against Lang's financial policies and agitate for the Riverina to become a separate state. The New England movement was the most long-lasting and determined, with an unsuccessful plebiscite to form the new state held as recently as 1967.

The other persistent challenge to the federal compact in the 1930s was from Western Australia, which had been the last and most reluctant member of the federation. With its economy largely reliant on the export of primary commodities, Western Australians resented the national policy on tariffs, which favoured manufacturing in the eastern states. And they were a long way away: it was 2695 kilometres by road from Perth to Adelaide and 3723 to Canberra; Perth was about as far away from the east coast of Australia as New Zealand. The collapse of the price of wheat in the early 1930s hit Western Australia hard. The historian Geoffrey Bolton has argued that rather than sharpening class conflicts, the tensions of the Depression were displaced onto the eastern states, whose extravagance, symbolised by the new capital in Canberra, and radicalism were seen as contributing to Western Australia's woes. In April 1933, at the end of a long, hot summer, two-thirds of Western Australians voted to secede from the federation. The referendum came to nothing, as the British parliament refused to dissolve WA's compact with the federation without the Commonwealth's agreement.

The idea of secession remained a potential focus for political grievance. In 1974 the iron ore magnate Lang Hancock proposed it again, as hysteria grew over the Whitlam government and its minister Rex Connor's threat to intervene in the mining industry. In 1993, addressing a dinner of the Samuel Griffith Society, the premier, Sir Richard Court, assured the audience that

> the secession sentiment is alive and well in Western Australia today … We have 9 per cent of Australia's population but produce a quarter of our nation's exports. We are self-sufficient in all essentials of life and major net exporters of agricultural products, minerals and petroleum.

Court made clear that he was not an advocate of secession, but he was certainly sympathetic to Western Australia's case for a better deal within the federation, an argument that has gained strength with the extraordinary mining boom of the past decade. The Liberal premier, Colin Barnett, is fighting federal Labor on this basis, rejecting the redistribution of income from mining that he believes the government is imposing on his state. He kept Western Australia out of Rudd's attempted health agreement and has fought the mining tax. "I don't believe that much of the rest of Australia, including the federal bureaucracy, actually understands this state and what is happening here," he told the *Australian*'s Paul Kelly. And he deeply resents the way the east looks down on Western Australia as little but a quarry, reliant on a hillbilly dig-it-up, ship-it-out economy, oblivious to the scale and technical sophistication of contemporary mining operations. This is what the current fight over the GST is all about, with Barnett complaining that Western Australia is being asked to pay too much. "We can accept that we share this prosperity," he said, "particularly as for most of the post-war period the other states subsidised WA." But he wants Western Australia to keep 75 cents of each dollar, not 68 cents as on current calculations. Otherwise, he threatened, Western Australia will secede by stealth, engaging more and more with Asia and letting relations to the east slide into irrelevance.

In 2010 old fissures in the federation re-emerged, fault-lines of difference in identity and economic interest. Not only was this seen in the election of the country independents, but also in the sharp differences in voting patterns across the states. The election did not have the usual relatively uniform national swing; instead states voted their own way. In Western Australia Labor won only 3 of the 15 federal seats; in Queensland 8 out of 30. In Victoria, by contrast, it won 22 of 37; in South Australia 6 of 11; and in Tasmania the Coalition won none. The breakaways were Western Australia and Queensland, rich with resources and voting against the traditional party of bigger government. The old manufacturing states of South Australia, New South Wales and Victoria on the whole stuck with Labor, though only just, as once safe seats were transformed into marginals. And Tasmania, too, stuck with the party most sympathetic to government-led amelioration of inequality. The uneven pattern of support has continued into this year. In a February *Age*/Nielsen poll, Labor was well ahead in Victoria on the two-party-preferred, but in Queensland it was well behind at 39–61.

There is a story here about the parties, in particular about the decline of the Country/National Party as an effective and credible representative of non-metropolitan interests, which I will discuss later. There is also a story about the federation, and shifting balances of economic power among the states. These, however, are part of a much larger story about long-term changes to the Australian economy and the shift in the balance of power between the country and the city, between non-metropolitan and metropolitan Australia. With the neoliberal reforms of the 1980s – what became known in Australia as "economic rationalism" – once-accepted arguments about the contribution of country people to the nation were dismissed by policy-makers as so much special pleading, and the subsidies provided for rural life were whittled away, leaving many people outside the capital cities feeling abandoned and betrayed.

Social changes have compounded the effects of economic change. When I was growing up in the 1950s, like many of my friends I had country cousins. We were children of the sons and daughters of farming families. Born in the 1920s and 1930s, watching their parents struggle through the 1930s, after the war our parents sought their future in the cities. On holidays, though, we went to the farm, visiting grandparents, aunts and uncles, and learned something of what the world looked like from the farm gate. And in school we all learned of the importance of rural industries to Australia. We pasted bits of wool into our project books and watched jerky educational films on the wheat industry, concrete silos towering against hard blue skies and golden grain pouring into waiting rail trucks. That was over half a century ago. Today, when I teach the politics of rural Australia to university students, only a few have connections with the country. They know about it from the media, but they have little understanding of its history and are far more likely to fly to the beaches of Bali or Queensland for their holidays than to spend them in Melbourne's rural hinterland.

City and Country in Australia share a history, a long history both of interdependence and of watchful suspicion. The understanding of that interdependence was strong in the first two centuries of Australia's European settlement, and the attempt to build a vibrant and self-sustaining countryside was a major political preoccupation. The country made claims on the city for support, and by and large the city attempted to meet them as part of a compact in which Australians shared the cost of living in a big country. This understanding has waned rapidly since the neoliberal 1980s. Since then the country has seemed to be in a perpetual state of crisis: dying towns, depressed and ageing farmers, unproductive farms carrying too much debt, environmentally unsustainable irrigation schemes, droughts and flooding rains, crisis-ridden marketing schemes like the wool stockpile and the Australian Wheat Board, and so on. The picture is of irreversible decline. Yet, as Tony Windsor reminds us, over 30 per cent of Australians live outside the big cities. What is their role in the nation? And what are we to do with all that land beyond the ranges and the thinly settled coastal strip? To begin to think about these questions, we need to take a long view and understand the history of the interrelationship between city and country in Australia, how this has shaped our political institutions and our political culture, and how and why it has changed. We need to understand all this if we are to be in a position to assess the grounds for a new compact between country and city in Australia in the twenty-first century.

THE SIXTH PILLAR

In the introduction to his book *The End of Certainty*, Paul Kelly puts forward a powerful framework for understanding the political and economic changes in Australia in the 1980s. These involved the dismantling of what he describes as the five pillars of the Australian Settlement. In this settlement, manufacturers were given protection from import competition, and workers a fair and reasonable wage determined by arbitration. The trade-off was as follows: manufacturers could have protective tariffs if they paid their workers a fair and reasonable wage. In the famous Harvester ruling, so called because it was to settle a dispute over payment to workers making Sunshine Harvesters, Justice Higgins determined a fair and reasonable wage on the basis of the cost of living, without consideration of the company's capacity to pay. This severance of wages from productivity basically held until the 1980s, when an ALP government introduced productivity-based wage gains.

To these two pillars of protective tariffs and wage arbitration, Kelly adds state paternalism, White Australia and reliance for defence on a powerful friend and ally, first Great Britain and then the United States. These, he claims, were the policy assumptions which developed in the two decades after federation, which underpinned Australian policy until the 1970s and 1980s, and which were dismantled in the 1980s and 1990s by the Hawke/Keating governments and by sympathetic state governments.

Aspects of Kelly's argument have been overtaken by events; in particular, Australia has not maintained the independent-mindedness in foreign policy which Kelly saw emerging in the 1980s. We followed the US into war in Afghanistan in much the same way as we had followed it into Vietnam. But the core argument has held: Australia has developed a more open, less regulated economy; tariffs have been dismantled; productivity and enterprise bargaining have become key factors in wage setting; and government has shifted some of its functions to the market. The privatisation since the 1980s of state-owned enterprises reminds us of the ubiquity of government in the provision of services before the 1980s: Qantas, TAA (Trans-Australia Airlines), public transport networks, power utilities and banks. Privatisation has gone further in some states than others, with Victoria under Jeff Kennett in the 1990s a particularly enthusiastic divestor of government-owned enterprises, and the NSW state government only now moving to sell off its electricity producers and suppliers. The report card is mixed. Privatisation has certainly achieved one of its main aims, which was to break the power of key public sector unions in the power and transport industries. However, when the trains fail, a government still gets punished whether it owns them or not, as the Victorian Labor premier John Brumby discovered last year when he lost a swag of seats down the troubled Frankston train line and lost the election.

Kelly draws attention to the political ideas embedded in long-standing national policies, but he has almost nothing to say about the country, nor about the federation. His is the perspective from Canberra, with a focus on national policy settings and national governments. But most of the policies of interest to country people have been delivered by state governments, which at federation retained power over land and resources, as well as being responsible for most of the infrastructure and for the provision of services, like education, health and policing, which affect people's day-to-day lives. Nor was the country much in the frame for the Hawke/Keating governments as they used their Accord with the ACTU to lock the union movement into the deregulation of tariffs and the slow unwinding of industrial arbitration. Labor seemed barely to notice the country as it reeled from blow after blow to its subsidies and self-understanding. For there was a sixth pillar to the Australian Settlement, which was also built in the decades after federation and dismantled in the neoliberal 1980s. Like arbitration and protective tariffs it had a long history, embedded in policies and institutional structures, and underpinned by widely held ideas about the place of the country in the Australian nation. Just as with the trade-off between tariffs and wages, there was a trade-off between the country and the city, brokered and administered by government, to compensate country people for the costs of remoteness and sparse settlement, to give them a "fair share" of Australia's resources. And, just as with tariffs and arbitration, neoliberal policymakers systematically attacked the terms and conditions of the trade-off and the ideas embedded in it.

There is one important caveat to this sixth pillar: Australia's indigenous people, most of whom lived outside the cities, were not party to the trade-off. In a nation obsessed – as we will see – by population growth, Australia's indigenous people were not even counted in the census. Living in missions and reserves and on the fringes of country towns, they inhabited a sort of limbo, neither city nor country, on the edge of the nation's consciousness.

A big country

What was the trade-off about and why was it necessary? The answer is in Australia's daunting political geography. Australia is a very big country with a small population. Outside the capital cities the population is spread too thinly; and across much of the continent there's almost no one living at all. "A nation for a continent" was the promise of federation: a political community claiming and inhabiting its territory, with its citizens enjoying an equality of rights as members of a modern democracy. But it is very costly for governments to provide country dwellers with the same level of services as closely settled city dwellers. As well, in a political system based on single-member electorates, country dwellers risk having less political punch than populous metropolitan electorates. So how were Australians outside the capital cities and major regional centres to make their voices heard and ensure that their needs were met, such that they did not become second-class citizens? The answer is complicated, as it includes compensation by both state and federal governments, as well as trade-offs among the states. These were embedded in the conditions of the federation hammered out in the 1890s to help persuade reluctant colonies like Western Australia and Tasmania to join the new Commonwealth.

By the time of federation the pattern of Australia's population distribution was clear: most people lived in the south-eastern coastal fringe of New South Wales and Victoria, and in the south-west corner of Western Australia, and by world standards relatively more of us lived in cities. Optimistic dreams of reproducing the closely settled countryside of Britain, or of dispersing the population across the continent as in the US, foundered on Australia's very different geography. Across most of the continent the soil is too poor and the rainfall too low and too irregular to support a higher population density. By 1891 one-third of the Australian white population lived in settlements of 10,000 or more, and the colonial capitals were already dominating their states. At federation 36 per cent of the population of New South Wales lived in Sydney and 41 per cent of Victoria in Melbourne. Over the next fifty years or so, although the population of rural Australia remained constant at about 2 million people, it declined relatively from 40 per cent of the national population to around 21 per cent. And as rural areas had higher fertility rates, this decline was in good part because from the early 1900s many young country-born people left home for the bright city lights.

The drift to the cities stopped in about 1970. There has since been a slight drift back, mainly to the coastal areas of New South Wales and Queensland, and to the new mining areas. This population shift, however, has not reduced the cultural and economic power of Australia's cities; quite the contrary. The lifestyle communities of sea- and tree-changers remain city-focused, with many living off the proceeds of their years of city work. Until recently remote mining communities were independent of city-based social and economic rhythms, but the fly-in fly-out workforce has changed this, as the workforce commutes from the city. It is only in Queensland and Tasmania that the majority of the population lives outside the capital cities. No wonder the city interests dominate politicians' minds.

Nor has the slight shift of population away from cities since the 1970s reinvigorated many rural towns. The inland and the dry sheep and wheat belts are still losing population. Smaller towns have shrunk as the so-called sponge cities have grown – regional centres such as Shepparton or Dubbo soaking up the small service towns of horse-and-buggy days and becoming hubs for government and commercial services. A combination of increased mobility and government policy has drained many smaller towns of purpose, marooning older residents and providing a rich reservoir for pathos in images of boarded-up shops and a few remnant locals with memories of grander days.

This problem of numbers is compounded by the huge distances. The cost per head of population of delivering services is obviously much more expensive than in the closely settled cities. And, as this past summer has made us only too aware, people living in the country are more exposed to the vicissitudes of nature in this wide brown land of drought, fire and flooding rains, their livelihoods and even their lives more at risk from natural disaster.

In the 1920s and 1930s various mechanisms were established to protect the political interests of people living outside the capital cities and to moderate the differences in standard of living: adjustments to the electoral system; cross-subsidisation of government services; fiscal equalisation between the states; government-sponsored schemes to support rural producers.

Tony Windsor's complaint that the 2010 election was fought out in the western suburbs of Sydney is a contemporary version of an old refrain. Country people have long believed that their interests are neglected by city-based politicians chasing the more numerous city votes and courting powerful big-city interests. In consequence, methods were devised to protect rural representation, such as allowing country electorates to have many fewer voters, or drawing electoral boundaries to skirt large regional towns where Labor voters would dilute the expression of rural interests. Country members consistently opposed adjustments to rebalance rural and urban electorates.

Most of this protection has now gone. The Whitlam government delivered a body blow to rural representation when it reduced the allowable difference between country electorates from 20 per cent above or below the quota to 10 per cent, effectively reducing the permissible difference in the size of electorates from 40 per cent to 20 per cent. With this change, said Whitlam, "We shall be ensuring that the number of voters in each electorate is much closer than it is now to the ideal of equality." He quoted Chief Justice Warren of the Supreme Court of the United States of America in 1964: "The weight of a citizen's vote cannot be made to depend on where he lives. A citizen – a qualified voter – is no more or no less so because he lives in the city or on the farm." In the bitter politics of brinkmanship leading up to the 1974 election, the Country Party had been desperate to stop this change, but without success. Even so, the change had little immediate impact as country Australia rallied against the socialists in Canberra. In 1984 the Hawke government introduced one-vote one-value electoral boundaries, but because the National Party argued successfully that this should be implemented by increasing the number of lower house seats rather than by a redistribution, again there was no immediate impact. Nevertheless, this was only a slight stay in the Nationals' long-term electoral decline: from twenty-one seats in 1984 with 10.6 per cent of the vote to ten seats with 5.49 per cent of the vote in 2007.

The federal constitution also protects the interests of the more sparsely settled states, guaranteeing the six original states five lower house seats. With a population of around 500,000, Tasmania has five seats; by contrast, with a population of 345,000, the largely urban ACT has only two electorates. Then there's the Senate, with all the states, no matter what their population, having twelve senators. Tasmania's population of 500,000 thus has the same number as New South Wales's almost 7 million. Rural voters were also protected at the state level. Queensland's gerrymandering and malapportionment was the most notorious. During the 1980s, as Queensland's population swelled with sun-seekers from Victoria and New South Wales, the National Party government under the leadership of Joh Bjelke-Petersen benefited from redistributions which reduced the importance of Brisbane as against the rest of Queensland.

Until the neoliberal 1980s and 1990s, the state and federal governments were monopoly providers of many basic services and much infrastructure, making cross-subsidisation through taxation and pricing mechanisms a relatively simple matter. At federation the Postmaster General's Department (PMG) was given control of postal, telegraphic, telephonic "and other like services," with the obligation to provide these to remote areas. These new forms of communication promised to conquer distance for people living in Australia's remote and scattered communities, to knit them more closely into the nation and increase their access to basic services like health and education. The government was expected to provide the access, and not charge full cost. The two living descendants of the PMG, Australia Post and Telstra, still carry a version of that obligation. Australia Post is required to carry a standard letter for a uniform price anywhere in Australia; and Telstra is bound by a universal service obligation to ensure that all people in Australia, no matter where they live, have reasonable access on an equitable basis to standard telephone services and payphones. Broadband is simply the latest in a long line of promised technological fixes to the tyranny of Australia's distances. People in the bush want the NBN, says Tony Windsor, "because it negates location and distance."

Similarly, railways and irrigation schemes, established in part to support closer settlement on the land, made huge losses that disappeared into the consolidated accounts. The extent of these subsidies was apparent by the 1920s and 1930s, but there was little political interest in finding a remedy, evidence not only of the political clout of rural interests but also of the widely held belief that supporting the country was worth the price. State-owned enterprises subsidised the country in another way: they provided tens of thousands of jobs and contributed to the viability of many towns. Every district had a post office and telephone exchange, a postmaster or mistress and someone to connect locals' calls to the next exchange, and, if they were that way inclined, to listen in to the conversation. The old PMG employed postmen, mail sorters, linesmen, telephonists and technicians right across the country and was Australia's largest national employer, as was its successor Telecom. The power companies and water utilities similarly provided thousands of skilled and semi-skilled manual jobs.

The Commonwealth also devised ways to redistribute its tax take among the states, in what is called "horizontal fiscal equalisation." An awkward technical term, it means spreading tax revenue so that no matter where Australians live, they are provided with a minimum standard of services. It was one of the ways of making good Australia's commitment to regional equality, ensuring that everyone got their fair share of the country's wealth.

Obviously it was more expensive for the governments of Queensland and Western Australia to provide services to their populations scattered over huge distances than for the governments in the more closely settled south-eastern states, yet before the minerals boom of the 1960s they had far less revenue per head. Redistributing Commonwealth taxes among the states began with federation and was systematised in 1933 when the Commonwealth Grants Commission was established to ensure equality of provision. The Grants Commission was a response to the potential political fracturing of the federation in the early 1930s, in particular secessionist Western Australia. Horizontal fiscal equalisation also involves a transfer from the city to the country – from the urban populations of Sydney and Melbourne, in particular, to their country cousins in the other states. In 1999 the two recipients, Tasmania and the Northern Territory, were also Australia's two least urbanised zones.

There were also various devices to support agricultural producers, small farmers in particular. Sugar, fruit and dairy were protected by tariffs and import quotas. And statutory marketing boards were established from the 1920s onwards across the range of agricultural sectors: wool, wheat, dairy and so on. The idea was simple: a combination of producers would be able to get a better price, providing a countervailing power to the big purchasers and eliminating middlemen. These boards were more than voluntarist cooperatives; established by law, they regulated markets in agricultural produce. For example, only eggs which had been graded, tested and stamped by the various state Egg Boards could lawfully be sold, consigning backyard egg producers to barter or under-the-table exchanges. A friend whose mother kept a well-populated backyard chook pen in the 1950s remembers the furtiveness accompanying the exchange of eggs for money in his otherwise respectable and law-abiding household. Some boards also supported the cost of research and promotional activity. The stand-out example here is the Australian Wool Board. As artificial fibres overtook the wool market in the 1950s, it assiduously promoted the virtues of wool for the garment industry, inventing the Woolmark logo as a guarantee of quality. In some cases the boards bought the produce from the grower at a guaranteed price and organised the export. This is the origin of the Australian Wheat Board's single desk. Just as with the labour movement, for farmers, too, unity was strength and they sought protection from market forces through state regulation. Country Party socialism again.

The country supported its claims to special treatment with three main arguments. First, Australian exports were almost entirely rural, with the economy riding on the sheep's back until at least the 1950s. Second, to be a nation and defend its claim to the continent, Australia needed to fill up its empty spaces with people who were prepared to live away from the comfort and convenience of cities. And third, country people made a larger contribution to the nation's distinctive and characteristic virtues than did city dwellers. The last of these, as we will see, is classic agrarianism and on its own was unlikely to have won the country special treatment. It may have given comfort to country people doing it hard to believe that they were more virtuous than others, but the city would have soon become inured to rural moral preening and whinging demands for special treatment were it not also perceived to be in its own interests to keep people on the land.

The sheep's back

The first and overwhelmingly convincing claim that the country could make for special treatment was economic. This is well known, but it is still worth rehearsing because it is the key to understanding the political power the country once had and why this has evaporated. Australia became one of the world's wealthiest countries in the nineteenth century because of sheep. Gold helped, but it was the export of fine wool that drove the economy. This was a New World phenomenon. In almost all other developed nations, prosperous modern economies were built through industrialisation – that is, by shifting labour and capital from low-productivity agriculture to high-productivity manufacturing, an often slow and painful process as villagers and peasants were turned into an industrial working class. But in the settler societies of Australia, the US, Canada, Argentina and New Zealand, economic growth and high incomes were based on rural production. Land was cheap and plentiful, and farming methods were unencumbered by traditional methods and labour relations.

Rural exports provided far more more than access to foreign currency. Much of the economic activity of the cities came from the links they provided between the rural hinterland and the world. Australian cities as they developed in the nineteenth century were ports, transport hubs and service centres through which farmers and pastoralists shipped their produce to the world economy. Nineteenth-century Australians did not settle in large numbers on the coast because they liked the beach, but because this was where the ships came in. Said Prime Minister Billy Hughes in 1921, putting a man on the land "provides a job for one man and probably two men in the city."

Although some sectors of agriculture (mainly dairy, sugar and dried fruit) benefited from subsidies, for the most part Australian agriculture was highly efficient. This very efficiency, though, was a problem: raising, shearing, sorting and transporting the golden fleece did not produce enough jobs for a population of much more than three or four million. Nor did Australia want to stay as a mainly agricultural economy; it aspired to modern industrial development. But how was this to be achieved in a country with high labour costs and a small market? Australian industrialisation has rarely been able to achieve self-sustaining momentum. Rather it has been slow, protracted and dependent on shelter from competition.

Tariffs on imports redistributed national income from highly productive agriculture to less productive and globally uncompetitive manufacturing, and although pastoral interests would complain, most Australians regarded this to be in the interests of the nation as a whole. Why? Until the 1980s and 1990s the debate about tariffs and protection was not primarily about economics, but about what sort of society Australia was to be: a society with a few wealthy landholding families running hugely profitable businesses exporting wool, or a more populous society offering a decent life to many, many more people. Protection of industry was a nation-building strategy, to provide jobs for an expanding population.

A nation for a continent

This was the promise of federation, a political community coterminous with Australia's vast territory. But to make it happen, Australia needed more people. It was a truism for the men and women of the first half of last century that vast, empty Australia needed to be filled with people, and that the people should be white. By the beginning of the twentieth century the land was mapped and settled, but Australians were acutely aware of the smallness of their population in relation to the hugeness of their continent and the heavily populated regions to their north, whose denizens were believed to look this way with hungry eyes. From the beginning of settlement people had been brought here by governments: some as unwilling prisoners for convict colonies and others as assisted immigrants. Governments and private associations also worked hard to attract free immigrants. Australia needed more people, not just to expand its internal workforce and domestic market, but also to fill up its uninhabited areas, in particular the centre and the north.

Defence, too, required that the people be spread across the land. As the Queensland poet George Essex Evans wrote before World War I,

> How shall we make Australia great
>   And strong when danger calls
> If half the people of the State
>   Are crammed in city walls ...?

The urgency of this was strongest after each of the two world wars, when the sense of national vulnerability was understandably high. In 1923 the prime minister, Stanley Melbourne Bruce, told an Imperial Economic Conference that "Australia's aim above everything else is to populate her country and advance from her position of a very small people populating a very vast territory." And after World War II Australians were warned that they must "Populate or perish." This catchy alliterative slogan, first used by Billy Hughes between the wars, was designed to etch the link between increased population and strategic security on the popular imagination.

Until the 1950s, governments attempted not only to increase the population but to encourage it to spread across the country. Cheap land was one of the lures to entice migrants to cross the globe, and from the 1860s onwards government reforms attempted to redistribute the large pastoral runs to more numerous settlers and their families. The family farm, not the squatter's station, was to be the ideal dwelling of rural Australia, for no matter how profitable the pastoral industry, underpopulated sheep runs were not regarded as a sufficient basis for a nation; far better a countryside filled with independent yeoman farmers. Soldier-settlement schemes followed both world wars, as policy-makers sought to remove returned men from the political and social temptations of the city and turn them into property-owning farmers. This motivation was strongest in the troubled years after World War I, when returned soldiers were seen as potential recruits to radical causes.

Settling new families on the land, however, required massive government spending. To begin with, from the 1890s existing owners had to be compensated for land acquired and the new farmers lent money for stock, fencing, machinery and housing. Then the new communities had to be provided with infrastructure and services: roads and railways to transport the goods to the ports and towns; irrigation schemes; power and telecommunications; schools and hospitals. These schemes did expand and diversify the farming sector, building dairying and horticulture in particular, but the cost to the public purse was huge. State governments borrowed massively from the London money markets to fulfil the dream of a densely settled countryside. These public debts contributed to Australia's woes when the Depression hit.

The cost was not only to the public purse; it was also paid in the hard work and heartbreak of the many men and women who were unable to make a go of it. British migrants lured to the south-west corner of Western Australia during the 1920s by the promise of free land and rural family life faced virgin forest which had to be cleared by hand before any crops could be sown. Many lasted only a few years. In Victoria over 60 per cent of settlers had left their farms by the time war broke out again, defeated by drought, rabbits and the falling commodity prices of the Depression.

Many settlers were on the land because the government had effectively placed them there. As the historian Keith Hancock observed in the 1930s: "The settlers, remembering that the Government had put them there, not infrequently imagined that it had in some way or other accepted an obligation to keep them there." The Country Party leader Jack McEwen, who became a soldier-settler in Victoria's Goulburn Valley when he was nineteen, agreed. It was an irrigation district that did not have enough irrigation. Nor did the settlers have enough land or capital. "All of these things were within the authority of the government: to give us more land; to give us more capital; to give us more water and so on." So McEwen joined with other soldier-settlers to put their case to government.

The cost of closer settlement was also paid by the land itself, cleared and overstocked, its fertility declining rapidly and its topsoil blowing away. During the 1920s, the heyday of Australia Unlimited in the optimistic years before the Depression, some imagined that the continent could support a population of 100 million, even 500 million, and doubters were regarded as unpatriotic. One vocal doubter, the geographer Griffith Taylor, was all but run out of Australia for using the words "arid" and "desert" to describe the inland, and for arguing that much of the land being opened up for closer settlement could not sustain intensive farming. He predicted that the Australian environment would restrict population growth to around 20 million by the turn of the century and was roundly abused as a "determinist." In a precursor of the debate between science and the climate change deniers, Taylor's opponents imported a Canadian "possibilist," Vilhjalmur Stefansson, to investigate Australia's deserts and marginal regions and counter Taylor's pessimism.

Stefansson was well known for propounding imaginative settlement possibilities for the world's cold deserts and was equally optimistic about the hot ones: "The worthlessness of any large territory is imaginary ... The reclaiming of the waste spaces of the world is merely a matter of the growth of education concerning them." Large areas of central Australia, he concluded, were suitable for extensive sheep-raising. By contrast, Taylor attacked the cherished beliefs of the day – the White Australia policy, the extension of railways through the arid interior, denser settlement of land with low rainfall, and the development of the tropical north – and was hounded for it. The University of Western Australia even banned his books. In 1928, fed up with Australia's insularity, he resigned from his post at the University of Sydney and took up a professorship in Chicago.

After World War II, closer settlement schemes were again embarked on, though they were not so extensive and were much better planned than those following World War I, with attention paid to the farming skills and business acumen needed for people to make a go of it on the land. The failure of the World War I schemes, together with the rural hardship of the Depression, marked the end of the dream that small family farms could fill Australia with people. If the choice was between the economic goal of efficient agriculture and the social goal of more people on the land, post-war Australia chose efficient agriculture, a choice it has had to make again and again – and is still making.

Even so, confident post-war planners still believed they could intervene to stop the drift to the cities. Incentives were given to industry to relocate manufacturing capacity and major power developments to areas such as Victoria's Latrobe Valley and New South Wales' Hunter Valley, Illawarra and Lithgow regions. Decentralisation was widely supported during the 1950s. As one proponent put it in 1954, "Without such a policy Australia will cease to be a nation, and will become a collection of City-States perched precariously round the edge of a de-populated bread bowl."

Legends

The third argument country people made to support their claim to special treatment was that they contributed disproportionately to the character of the nation, both to its distinctiveness and its moral character. The push for settlement had been driven not just by the need to fill the empty land, but also by the yeoman ideal, the belief that it was better for people to live in the country than the city, that a nation filled with hard-working, independent farming families would be a better, stronger nation than a nation of soft-bellied city dwellers.

In 1918 the Victorian newspaper *The Leader* warned that "The aggregation of cities is like a wen, which draws an injurious sustenance at the expense of the general vitality." This was agrarianism, a set of beliefs about the primacy of agriculture in human society that rests on three claims: that rural life is more natural and virtuous than city life; that everyone depends on the food produced by farmers; and that farmers are particularly hard-working and independent people and so more morally worthy than many city dwellers. Part of this is captured by a Victorian Country Party MP interviewed in the late 1950s: "I hope I'm not being parochial if I say that we stand for the most vital part of the economy that provides the exports and the best part of the food and clothing for the rest of the community."

Agrarianism's claim that the simple life of the countryside lived close to nature is morally superior to life in the hectic, overcrowded, sophisticated city had been picked up and transformed in the early nineteenth century by European nationalism, which looked to the country for traditions and ways of life uncontaminated by foreign and aristocratic rule. The simple lives of peasant folk were invested with a national significance. In English, the word "country" can refer both to the non-metropolitan areas and to the nation or territory as a whole, so it has always been easy to slide from country dwellers to true patriots. The dynamic in the New World was slightly different, although with the same result that the country rather than the city was where one looked for the true face of the nation.

America, Canada, Australia and New Zealand all have pioneering myths in which men and women are transformed from immigrants to nationals through their struggle with the land and their adaption to the new environment.

For the growing Australian nationalism at the end of the nineteenth century, the real Australia was the country. The people there had been shaped by the struggle with the unique problems of the Australian environment, and so made what they were by Australia. They were the bearers of the qualities of resourcefulness, endurance and laconic, courteous good humour which were widely seen as national attributes. Cities and city dwellers, by contrast, were much the same the world over, and so had made no special contribution to a distinctively Australian character.

Russel Ward summed this up in 1958 as the Australian Legend and put itinerant male bush workers at the centre of the national story. Ward described the "typical Australian," in terms still recognisable today, as an idealised male – practical, easygoing, rough-and-ready in his manners, suspicious of authority, proud of his independence, loyal to his mates, with a fondness for beer, gambling and swearing and a reluctance to submit to the domestication of matrimony. We're not talking here about what most Australian men are or ever were like, but about a type that has been taken to be representative for the past hundred years or so. Ward argued it began with the convicts, Australia's earliest bush workers, and was well established by the middle of the nineteenth century when the gold-rush immigrants arrived. It reached its apotheosis in the rural workers of the 1880s and 1890s, the shearers, drovers and boundary riders who formed Australia's first national unions and whose working lives provided the material for its best known folk songs – "Click Go the Shears," "The Drover's Dream," "Waltzing Matilda" and a host of others popularised in the bush-band revival of the 1970s by groups such as the Bushwhackers. The World War I correspondent Charles Bean saw the same qualities in the men of the First AIF, the Anzacs who drank and fought and caught VD in the brothels of Egypt, refused to salute the stuck-up British officers but proved to be brilliant soldiers. Through the Anzac legend Bean generalised the bushman's virtues across the armed forces, making it a wider model for Australian masculine behaviour and male bonding.

Ward was a communist who wanted to believe that the Australian national type was naturally socialist. But he was dreaming. In the 1950s, when *The Australian Legend* was published, Australians routinely returned conservative governments. John Hirst argues that the Australian Legend has a rival rural legend, the Pioneer Legend. This includes not just the itinerant rural labourers but the small farmers, wresting a living from the land with their courage, hard work and stoic perseverance, and their resourceful and hospitable wives. Hirst's version is tamer than Ward's, with the swearing and drinking cut out, but this legend is more inclusive of the experience of country people and has proven surprisingly durable.

In a much-quoted article, the political scientist Don Aitkin coined the term "countrymindedness" to describe the worldview of country Australia. The term originated with the Country Party itself, perhaps with its first national leader, Earle Page, who, when he first stood for federal parliament in 1919, described himself as "straight-out country." It sums up what is in effect a political ideology, "a system of values and ideas that … presents a more or less extensive picture of the good society and of the policies and programmes necessary to achieve it; distinguishes goodies from baddies; accounts for the historical experience of a group; and appears as 'truth' to that group while being at least plausible to outsiders."

With the three arguments I have outlined above, countrymindedness placed the country and agriculture at the centre of Australia, and on this basis pushed their claims for support. "Country Party socialism" is what its opponents called it, and it was at least special pleading. But to country people and their political representatives it was neither of these things. It was a well-justified demand that they be given their due on the basis of the contribution they made to the nation, a contribution far greater than their numbers and without which Australia could scarcely claim to be a nation at all.

THE COMPACT DISSOLVES

Off the sheep's back

Since World War II we have seen the second part of the story: the dissolving of the conditions that made the city willing to compensate the country. World War II was the watershed, when the focus of Australian nation-building shifted decisively from the country to the city, from agriculture to industrialisation. Before 1939, Australian manufacturing was relatively underdeveloped, concentrated in food, clothing and textiles. There was a steel industry; however, Australia imported most of its complex manufactured goods. Cars were put together here, but from mostly imported parts. When war broke out, Australia couldn't even make the optical glass needed for telescopes, binoculars, periscopes and range-finders. Manufacturing capacity had to expand rapidly indeed to produce the machines and equipment needed to fight a war: guns, tanks, ships, aircraft, trucks, scientific equipment, chemicals and so on. Australia's scientific capacity also grew rapidly, as did its skilled engineering workforce. This was the point when secondary and tertiary industries overtook agriculture in terms of share of GDP and of employment.

The massively increased manufacturing capacity and scientific know-how developed during the war provided a solid basis for industrial growth, so long as two crucial shortages could be overcome: labour and capital. The solution was to import them both. Migrant workers would be employed in new factories, which would be built by foreign capital. Multinationals would be lured to invest in Australia because tariffs would ensure them protected access to a domestic market. Post-war migration brought in not only workers, but consumers, people who would need to build a house, buy clothes and furniture, and, when they could afford it, a car. When this was combined with the pent-up domestic demand after the Depression and then the war, the economy roared along. Real wages rose, by almost 4 per cent a year from 1949 to the end of the 1960s.

Agriculture, too, was booming, with high prices for wool and wheat, and buoyant demand. Country towns experienced something of a heyday, as country people bought cars and spent their rising incomes on the new consumer goods. But agriculture's share of the national economy was declining, and with it the claim of farmers and country people to be the economic backbone of the nation. Also declining inexorably was agriculture's share of world trade, and this spelled long-term trouble for the Australian economy. Whereas primary products had made up two-thirds of world trade in the nineteenth century, by 1966 they were one-third and by 1983 only 17 per cent – far, far outstripped by trade in goods and services. Even as Australia seemed at its most prosperous after the war, it was being marginalised as a trading nation, its share of world trade declining from 2.5 per cent in 1946 to 1.1 per cent in 1997.

The decisions policy-makers took in the early years after the war had crucial consequences for the Australian economy. Rather than building a manufacturing sector oriented to export, Australia went down the path of import substitution. For cars, white goods, clothes and machinery, we would "buy Australian," even if it cost us a little bit more. This strategy is only possible for countries that can generate export income from another source. It created a dual economic structure – with one part of the economy exposed to the uncertainties and competition of world trade and forced to be adaptive, resilient and competitive; and the other focused on the cities, inward-looking, insulated from competition and dependent for innovation on imported R&D. There was a certain truth to many country people's belief that the city was soft, filled with public servants and trade unionists who would get paid regardless of the weather or world commodity prices.

After the 1960s, minerals replaced wool as Australia's export staple, a lucky escape, as artificial fibres rapidly reduced the price for fine wool. By 1970 wool, which had provided 47 per cent of Australia's export income in 1950, contributed only 15 per cent of Australia's gross agricultural production. No longer on the sheep's back, Australian prosperity now rode on the top of railway trucks full of coal, and alumina and iron ore. This was a major re-balancing of Australia's export industries, but it did not shift the reliance on non-metropolitan economic activity and on the people who lived and worked outside the comfortable cities. Mining, however, is an unstable basis for permanent settlements, based on the extraction of a non-renewable resource. And although it can provide an effective substitute for agriculture in the country's balance of trade, its capacity to support rural communities is marginal.

The emptying land

As agriculture's economic importance declined, so did the numbers of those living in the country. And furthermore, because Australia's agriculture is very efficient by world standards, fewer and fewer people were needed to produce the same amount. Thus, even as agriculture modernised and adapted to maintain its economic role, it undermined its capacity to fill Australia with people. Farm numbers have been declining since World War II. Farm work comprised 28 per cent of total employment in 1933, 15 per cent in 1954 and is now at around 4 per cent, with farmers and their spouses increasingly needing to take off-farm jobs to support their families. Although the vast majority of Australian farms are still family concerns, corporate farms account for an increasing acreage. There is thus a large gap between the economic output of the rural sector and its capacity to sustain rural towns and communities.

Debates about Australia's population still include strategic arguments, but these now focus on the size rather than the location of the population, and little attention is paid to the vastness of our thinly populated north and west. For example, Malcolm Fraser regularly puts forward a population target of 45–50 million for Australia if we are to avoid the envy and inevitable challenge of our poorer neighbours. He says nothing, though, about where this population should be located. There is little fear that any threat to Australia would come as a land-based invasion, so the location makes no real difference. The arrival of refugee boats in the north-west has focused attention on the long, unprotected coastline there, but it has not been accompanied by calls for denser coastal settlement, except by Bob Katter, who argues that his vast electorate of Kennedy could easily accommodate a population of 60 million.

Then there's the environment and the drastic revision that's been underway since the 1960s of our understanding of Australia's varied and unpredictable environment and the impact on it of two centuries of European farming practices. Two changes, in particular, have been profoundly unsettling for the country. The first is the rise of an environmental movement which values wilderness over agricultural land. The Victorian Little Desert campaigns of the late 1960s were met with disbelief by politicians who couldn't understand why people would fight to preserve straggly Mallee scrub when they could have cleared it to create pleasant and productive green pastures dotted with woolly sheep and contented cows. Although the big iconic environmental battles have been with the mining and timber industries and with the Tasmanian hydroelectricity commission over dams, these share with the campaigns to preserve bush and grasslands a move away from seeing nature predominantly in terms of immediate use value. Old-style agricultural country is no longer the taken-for-granted source of pride in the country's hard work and productivity which it was for earlier generations, but now also speaks of cleared forests and absent birds and mammals. Australia has more than 1500 species whose long-term survival is threatened, from the cute big-eyed bilbies to insects that we barely know exist. Habitat loss from land clearing is the biggest cause of species decline.

The second change is the profound doubts that have arisen about the long-term sustainability of European farming practices in Australian conditions. There is increasing evidence of serious degradation of the natural environment, for example in land salination, loss of soil cover and of biodiversity, and the deterioration of inland waterways. In the south-west of Western Australia, for example, it is estimated that by 2050 one-third of agricultural land will be severely damaged by dryland salinity, which is caused by the watertable rising in land that has been cleared of vegetation. Whereas previous governments encouraged clearing, they are now trying to reverse its effects and, in many cases, to re-vegetate. Irrigation also causes increased salinity as well as threatening the health of waterways, but the shocking but irrefutable fact is that without irrigation many inland towns would scarcely exist. As we have seen, in the final years of the drought Adelaide's water supply came under threat, with the Murray's declining water flows showing high salinity levels. Agriculture, the city, country towns and a host of threatened ecological systems are all competing for the same scarce resource.

Multicultural nation

Country Australia's place in the nation has been affected by another major change since World War II: the markedly increased ethnic diversity which has resulted from immigration. The increase in diversity has been greatest in the cities, because that is where most of the new migrants have settled. Between 1947 and 1996 the proportion of the rural population born over-seas increased from 7.6 per cent to 12.1 per cent, whereas the increase in urban areas was from 11.6 per cent to 29.2 per cent. Asian migrants, in particular, have shunned the country. Only 2.5 per cent of Vietnamese live outside the major cities, and 5.4 per cent and 5.1 per cent of people born in China and Hong Kong respectively. There are, of course, notable exceptions, such as the Italians in Griffith and Mildura, but on the whole the country stayed white while the city brindled. Country people visiting the city would play "spot the Aussie" and city folk would complain that you couldn't get a decent coffee in the country.

As the cities were socially and culturally transformed by migration, their residents started to argue that Australia's distinctiveness lay not in its resourceful, friendly country folk but in its ethnically mixed and culturally sophisticated capitals. For the first time Australian cities, especially Sydney and Melbourne, felt they could escape their status as provincial cities, much the same as provincial cities the world over:

Australia's distinctiveness could now derive from its success as a multicultural nation – in fact, it is often claimed to be the most successful multicultural nation in the world. And it is in the cities, not in the country, that this diversity is most to be found.

New attitudes to gender and race also led many city people to re-evaluate rural Australia. Hegemonic masculinity has persisted in the country far longer than in the city, aided by inheritance patterns in which less than 5 per cent of farms were bequeathed to daughters. The idealistic young students who rode the Freedom Bus with Charlie Perkins through the country towns of New South Wales in 1965 found them to be full of ugly, violent racists: some country dwellers even tried to run the bus off the road. During the 1970s, one strand of Australian cinema presented rural communities as home to all that is bad in Australian settler culture: racism, xenophobia, misogyny, intolerance and homophobia. In the 1971 film *Wake in Fright*, the core virtues of the Australian Legend are transformed into vices as a hapless young schoolteacher is captured by two outback characters and taken spotlighting kangaroos. He barely escapes with his sanity from the forced hospitality of their mateship and their violent displays of blokedom.

Henry Reynolds' 1981 work *The Other Side of the Frontier* marks another cultural turning point. Showing how Aboriginal people fought against what for them was an invasion, the book is a history of the violence of Australia's settlement. Other historians followed Reynolds, re-visiting the colonial period to reveal not a triumphal progress of peaceful settlement and nation-building, but a protracted and bloody frontier conflict that lasted into the twentieth century. Very little of this violence, however, took place in the cities, and city folk, who have had far less to do with indigenous Australians than people living in the country, found it relatively easy to include the experiences of indigenous Australians in their understanding of the nation's history. Nor, for the most part, did they feel threatened by land-rights and native-title claims, living on secure titles in areas from which all signs of indigenous occupancy had long been erased.

In the country it was a different story. After the *Mabo* judgment, farmers I knew chopped down and burned the scarred canoe tree next to their dam lest it help a native-title claim.

For the past three decades or so Australia's race, ethnic and gender politics have sharpened the urban/rural divide. This was most obvious in the city's response to Pauline Hanson and the One Nation Party in the late 1990s. No longer was it "What will they think in England?" – instead people worried about reactions in Singapore, New Delhi, Bangkok and Hong Kong, as Australia, always nervous of the spectre of White Australia, tried to make its way in the postcolonial world.

For much of the twentieth century, rural Australia had its own loud and effective political voice in the Country Party. Countrymindedness was its informing philosophy and a shrewd pragmatism its mode of operation as farmers-turned-politicians brought skills and ideas developed in managing farms to the management of the country. The Country Party has never been the sole representative of rural Australia, and many country electorates returned Liberal members, such as Malcolm Fraser's western district of Wannon. However, it was the specialist voice, able to put the view from the country unadulterated by the need to consider countervailing city interests and arguments, pushing the country's claims and reminding city dwellers how much they depended on the men and women on the land. It also put into parliament country men, farmers mainly, but also rural business owners and professional men, who would lobby hard for resources for their electorates and be effective go-betweens for their constituents with the faraway governments in Canberra and the state capitals.

Country dwellers are acutely aware of their distance from the centres of political power. Physical distance creates a companion sense of psychological and emotional distance, as Jennifer Curtin found when she interviewed people in five rural electorates in 2000 about their general experience of government and of political representation: "We feel that we are at the end of the line, forgotten. It's a tyranny of distance thing – being so far from Canberra. There are not a lot of us in rural areas any more, and we get overlooked"; "There is no sense of connection with parliament in Canberra. There is a feeling of isolation that we're here and they're way up there and somehow in some way what people would like to see happen is lost in that distance." The local member must provide the link, and Curtin also found that although the rural voters she spoke to distrusted government in general, they trusted and respected their local member. Said one, "Our local politician is very well respected in the community and has made quite big inroads back into the problems that this electorate had. The local politician is very attentive, works very hard, and is getting across a lot of the remote areas that weren't very well represented previously." All MPs have duties as local members, but expectations are especially high in country electorates, where people value local ties and face-to-face contact highly and where the parliamentarian is an important local identity. In big electorates, the local member is scarcely ever off the road or, nowadays, out of the plane.

Country parties were formed after World War I by various state-based farmers' organisations. They successfully pushed for the introduction of preferential voting, which enabled rival non-labour candidates to trade preferences and so avoid splitting the non-labour vote. At the 1922 federal election, fourteen representatives were elected from the Country Party. The new party held the balance of power, and soon showed that its support would not come cheap. Its parliamentary leader was Earle Page, a gifted surgeon from Grafton who had been a vigorous campaigner for a new state in northern New South Wales and was a passionate advocate for its development, if only it could get the bridges, rail, roads and hydro-electricity it needed to realise its potential.

Although he had been in parliament less than three years, Page made audacious political demands, refusing to take the party into a government led by Labor renegade Billy Hughes, whom he loathed. A humiliated and angry Hughes was forced out, and a coalition government was formed, led by the wealthy Melbourne businessman and returned soldier Stanley Melbourne Bruce. Nervous that the Country Party would be swamped by its larger and more experienced partner, Page persuaded Bruce to give it five of the eleven Cabinet positions, including treasurer and postmaster general. Polling a little over one-tenth of the national vote, with fourteen seats to its coalition partner's thirty-one, the Country Party was given almost half the ministries! Page became treasurer and deputy prime minister, and the government became known as the Bruce–Page government.

It is a mystery why Bruce agreed to such terms. He, too, was relatively new to the parliament, winning a by-election for the Victorian seat of Flinders in 1918 and spending a good deal of his time in politics running the family business. Perhaps he was too well mannered for a fight; or perhaps he was seeking to foster some political harmony amidst the bitter sectarian politics that were one of the legacies of the war and the two failed conscription referendums. Whatever the reason, this extraordinary deal, although subsequently wound back somewhat, enabled the Country Party to punch far, far above its weight for much of the twentieth century.

Rural politicians continued to play prominent roles in national and state politics until well into the 1980s. John McEwen, who became leader of the Country Party in 1958, was the second-best known politician of the Menzies era. Granite-faced, with jutting jaw and ramrod back, he had first entered federal politics in 1934, after sixteen years as a soldier-settler in northern Victoria battling drought, rabbits and falling prices like the rest of them. In 1974 he told an oral-history interviewer, "My early farm experience formed the basis of a lot of my views as leader of the Country Party." McEwen was a minister in coalition governments before the war, and then Minister for Commerce and Trade from 1949 until he retired from parliament in 1971, an extraordinary incumbency in which he championed protection and held at bay the growing numbers of doubters. McEwen was convinced that tariffs were needed to maintain employment and for strategic purposes, unpersuadable that jobs lost to manufacturing by removing protection would be replaced in the service industries. To him it was self-evident that the basic wealth-producing industries were agriculture, mining and manufacturing. Menzies' cabinets were full of men like him, born before World War I, who governed the post-war prosperity with political ideas formed in the hard inter-war years and took for granted that a prosperous, well-populated countryside was worth the price.

McEwen's successor as Country Party leader was good-looking young Doug Anthony, who had succeeded his father in the northern NSW seat of Richmond in 1957, when he was only twenty-seven. He became deputy prime minister as the Coalition government reeled from blunder to blunder and Whitlam's star rose, and after Whitlam's victory he was deputy leader of the Opposition. In 1973 he pushed through the party's name change from Country to National, which research had suggested would dilute the image of the party as a farmers' party and broaden its appeal in country towns. The Country-turned-National Party knew it was in long-term trouble, but the chaotic politics of the mid-1970s gave it a reprieve as non-labour rallied around traditional political values and ideas. Anthony was right by Malcolm Fraser's side as he pushed Whitlam towards the Dismissal. The election of 1975 returned the party's largest parliamentary membership ever: twenty-three MPs and eight senators, thirty-three balding Anglo men, with diversity provided by a few Catholics and Doug Anthony's full head of hair. Anthony and his fellow Nationals Peter Nixon and Ian Sinclair became senior members of Fraser's government, four farmers with a shared commitment to the country who thought Australia's mounting economic problems were the result of Labor mismanagement and inflation fuelled by trade-union wage demands. Like McEwen, Fraser's imagined economy was one of mines, farms and factories and he had little faith in the growing service economy. He wanted to free up regulation of the market, but it would be a market of bales of wool and bags of wheat, cars and shoes and truck-loads of coal, not a postmodern market of services and images and intellectual property and millions upon millions of cups of coffee.

When Fraser was defeated in 1983 and the national government passed to Labor, the economic and social changes that had been sidelining country Australia caught up with its politics. Out of power from 1983 to 1996 the Nationals faced impossible political choices, as their traditional ally, the Liberal Party, was not only in opposition but even more enthusiastic about the free market than Labor. As the Nationals' electoral base continued to shrink, the Liberals paid less and less heed to the country's interests. Yet if the Nationals were to leave the Coalition to champion continued protection of farmers and country people, they risked losing their place at the government table when Labor was eventually defeated, particularly if it was a landslide and the Liberals didn't need them. How would they then be able to win benefits for their rural electorates? As well, during the 1980s the National Farmers' Federation became a credible new voice for farmers. Unconstrained by parliamentary politics, it could lobby the Labor government just like any other sectoral pressure group or peak body.

The Nationals were saved from political irrelevance by indigenous politics. During the 1980s they joined forces with the mining industry to undermine and defeat the Labor attempt to introduce a uniform land-rights policy; and after the *Mabo* and *Wik* judgments they led the call for "bucket-loads of extinguishment" for any remnants of native title that had survived 200 years of European occupation. The Nationals were a godsend to the mining industry. Fighting to keep all of Australia open to exploration and development, mining was associated with the top end of town and had neither a social base to mobilise nor the capacity to pull city heart-strings. The Nationals could always find a farmer to hang over a gate and talk about his pioneering great-grandparents, his love for his family's farm, his care for the environment and how important the wheat he grew was for Australia's exports.

When the Coalition was re-elected in 1996, the Nationals drew various lines in the sand, such as on the full sale of Telstra, but their political influence continued to decline. Because they went along with the Liberals' enthusiasm for deregulation, they lost seats to country independents. As noted, in the 1970s the Country Party had averaged around 10 per cent of the federal vote and 22 seats in the House of Representatives. In 2007 it received 5.49 per cent and won 10 seats. The vote has risen and fallen with political events – Tim Fischer, who became leader in 1990, was able to revive its fortunes a little – but the long-term trend is down.

Fischer retired from the leadership in 1999 and subsequent National Party leaders have scarcely registered with the public. Tony Windsor complained about the 2010 election, "Where was Warren Truss?" An ex-National, he noticed his absence. Few others did. The Nationals are unlikely to disappear or to merge with the Liberals in the near future, but will continue as a small rural-based party with its main support in agricultural areas. Their vote at around 5 per cent is just a little more than the proportion of farmers and farm workers in the workforce. They are no longer able to represent the complex interests of the many other Australians who live outside the capitals and major regional cities, nor do they have the political and imaginative resources to negotiate a new national compact for the country. The question is: who does?

When the Coalition evicted the Whitlam government, it promised to restore Australia to the prosperity it had enjoyed in the long boom that had run for twenty years or so since the early 1950s. Unemployment levels nudging 4 per cent and inflation reaching a high of 17 per cent in 1975 were, according to Fraser and Anthony, the result of Labor's errors. With the right men back in charge of the country, all would be right. But it wasn't. The long post-war boom had ended. Stagflation, the joint appearance of unemployment and inflation, confounded economic policy-makers. Both unemployment and inflation continued to rise, and by 1980 Australia was in recession. In 1983, when the Coalition faced an election, unemployment was 10.3 per cent. The Coalition lost.

Back in power, Labor was determined to establish its economic credentials. New ideas were abroad about the need to rebalance markets and governments in the distribution of a nation's resources. The plan was for governments to get out of the way and let markets pick winners and restore prosperity. This was neoliberalism, and it posed a fundamental challenge to the large role government regulation played in Australia's highly regulated and relatively protected economy. Labor took up the challenge and set about opening up the Australian economy. As well, it took on a second challenge: to restructure the economy to find sources of export income beyond primary commodities. The combination pushed the country to the brink.

By the 1980s it was evident that the dual structure of the Australian economy was becoming unsustainable. The Hawke government embarked on a series of reforms designed to build a competitive export base: floating the dollar, reducing tariffs and modestly encouraging research and development. John Button's car plan hoped to save Australian car manufacturing by forcing it to rationalise and to export. Australia would no longer be a farm and a quarry, shipping wheat, wool and dirt to the rest of the world, but would build a modern, diversified export base, with a good share of the elaborately transformed manufactured goods which were the hallmark of a modern industrialised economy. This was Labor's modernising dream, and although it achieved a good deal, we now know that in essence it failed. The Australian economy is again prosperous, not because of strong export-oriented manufacturing but because the newly industrialising countries of Asia, especially China and India, are buying our minerals.

Under Hawke/Keating, Australian agriculture, too, would be made more competitive. Tariffs and quotas on produce were abolished or reduced, statutory marketing authorities dismantled and industry regulatory regimes simplified. A key argument was that there were too many farms. In large part this was the result of the policies of earlier governments, which had led to a proliferation of small family farms. But no matter: the social and political goals of filling the land with people were now irrelevant to the overriding economic goal of creating an efficient agriculture which did not rely on government subsidy. The main game was to increase agriculture's contribution to the national income. Oft-repeated statistics on farm viability reported that most of the profits in agriculture were made by the minority of enterprises large enough to benefit from economies of scale. A key aim of agricultural policy became to encourage owners of unviable farms to "exit the industry." "Get big or get out," farmers were told, and as financial markets were deregulated, many borrowed heavily to "get big," only to come to grief as interest rates were hiked in the late 1980s and early 1990s. Government would then mop up the social cost by helping the unprofitable "adjust."

Neoliberalism treated farms as businesses, and farmers as business owners and entrepreneurs. Farmers were told they were personally responsible for their farm's viability, and consequently for its failure. For example, in 1992 the National Drought Policy redefined drought, the bane of Australian farming, from a natural disaster to a risk which requires appropriate risk-management strategies. Drought-stricken farmers were no longer heroic victims of fickle nature, but merely bad risk managers. The new thinking stripped farmers of their previous cultural and nation-building roles and exposed many of them as not very good operators who had little choice but to leave. No wonder many farmers suicided.

To emphasise farmers' responsibility for the economic viability of their farms sits uncomfortably with a push for greater environmental awareness. Even though it makes long-term economic sense for farmers to adopt practices that will preserve the value of their land, short-term economic pressure can change priorities. Not surprisingly, when farmers are under economic stress, their commitment to environmental management wanes. Farmers just trying to stay afloat are far more likely to over-stock or to clear marginal land than farmers with fat margins. With its focus on economic productivity, neoliberalism has trouble with the commons, both social and natural.

The second blow to the country came from neoliberalism's bedfellow, the New Public Management, which inspired a radical rationalisation and restructuring of government service delivery. Just as national economies were to be transformed and revitalised by opening them up to competition and the entrepreneurial spirit, so too were the lumbering government bureaucracies, which had developed to deliver relatively equal services to Australian citizens wherever they lived, to be redesigned according to market principles. In Australia this included the large state-owned enterprises, many of which were privatised during the 1980s and 1990s: for example, gas and electricity companies, the Commonwealth Bank, public transport, airports and the two airlines. Other government enterprises, such as Australia Post, were corporatised. Rationalisation inevitably followed, as the requirement to make a profit forced the closure of unprofitable branches and user-pays became the order of the day. For example, between 1991 and 1997, following corporatisation, Australia Post reduced the numbers of post offices by around 25 per cent, many in rural areas where they were popular local meeting places. But such social functions couldn't be costed.

Treasuries and finance departments, intent on balancing budgets and producing surpluses, reined in the budgets of the service delivery departments, where most of the money is spent, and this had a disproportionate impact on rural services. The private sector followed suit. The most visible change was in banking, as main-street branches in their imposing historic buildings were downsized and eventually replaced by automatic tellers. Rural towns were dismayed. Since the founding of these towns, banks had brought in new families: bank managers to join the local golf club and chair fundraising drives, and tellers to play in the football team and marry their daughters. Now all they had was an ATM.

The waves of rationalisation that broke over rural Australia during the 1980s and 1990s have affected people living in the country in two main ways. First, and most obviously, there has been a decline in easy local access to many basic public services, such as health and education, which have now been centralised. The quality of services in many large regional centres has improved, with more universities and much better hospitals, but at the expense of smaller surrounding towns. This cost is most obviously borne by those who can't drive and must rely on family, friends or infrequent buses to transport them to the regional centres. Second has been the loss of jobs. The closing of post offices, banks, tele-communications and state rail depots, hospitals and schools, together with mergers of local councils, has had a multiplier effect. As govern-ment agencies and private businesses have individually pursued cost efficiencies, their decisions have impacted on each other to produce social outcomes for which no one takes responsibility – dying small towns and confused and distressed Australians who feel abandoned and betrayed.

Jennifer Curtin, who talked with rural voters in the early 2000s, reported a widespread feeling of being forgotten and unheeded. Said one, "People here are not against politics, they are all for democracy, they are all for the system we've got in Australia – it's been a good system – but there's that feeling of 'My voice isn't important' coming through." And another: "It wouldn't matter who is in there. It's the fact that it's so sparsely populated out this way means that when politicians come out, they promise the world – they say, 'Oh yes, we'll do this for such and such little community, isn't that wonderful.' But when they get back and they do their sums and 'Oh, we're going to get more votes if we do something somewhere else,' so they forget about us." In 1999 the Nationals leader John Anderson called his address to the National Press Club "One Nation or Two?" and claimed that "The sense of alienation, of being left behind, of no longer being recognised … for the contribution to the nation being made, is deep and palpable in much of rural and regional Australia today."

Earlier generations had acknowledged that regional inequalities were structural, the consequences of living in a big country with a sparse population, but in the neoliberal 1980s and 1990s regions were encouraged to take responsibility for their own futures by becoming more self-reliant, more entrepreneurial, more creative. There was some assistance with this, for example by providing leadership training, and there was much talk about the need to mobilise social capital, but the message was clear: don't look to government to bail you out; you're on your own. Like the farmers, regional communities were told they were responsible for their own future viability. What's more, they should stop complaining. A frustrated Tim Fischer told rural NSW paper The Land that he was "fed up with people saying the Government is doing nothing – it is. But rural communities must respond with courageous leadership and motivation." Addressing a forum on rural economic development in 1998, he made some suggestions: "Towns large and small must make their own way by maximising opportunities … Lockhart, verandah town; Crow's Nest, the only town with a true square; Broken Hill, world-renowned art colony." Tourism is the main strategy, boosted by a plethora of festivals to bring much-needed money into local economies. Music festivals like Tamworth, Gympie, Woodford and Port Fairy are huge and lucrative and there are hundreds of smaller ones, as well as wine and food, writers' and multicultural festivals. Some are organised by state ministries of the arts and community development, but many are home-grown. Wallington, on the Victorian Bellarine peninsula, has a strawberry festival; Goomeri, a town of only 500 souls to the west of Gympie, has a pumpkin festival; and Crookwell, in the southern tablelands of New South Wales, a potato festival. Pathos vies with inventiveness in these daggy celebrations of agricultural production and local history.

The speed of micro-economic reform increased in the second half of the 1990s, when the Council of Australian Governments agreed that all Australian governments would review and reform their laws to ensure that they did not restrict competition. It was then that I heard the retired National Party politician Bruce Evans make the statement that I have taken as a theme for this essay: "We all live in a big country and we should all share the cost." For Evans, and for many other country people, National Competition Policy became a symbol of the failure of state and federal governments and of city-based elites to understand the problems of the country as people paid more for services that were previously subsidised, or lost them altogether. To apply market principles to the provision of government services was to reject country Australia's historic sense of entitlement to special treatment, its belief that it was owed a "fair share." Or rather, it re-configured what a fair share meant as something that the market would determine.

Once the problems of the country were problems for the country as a whole. But then government stepped back to allow market forces and technological change to redistribute resources in the interests of economic efficiency, and made little specific commitment to country Australia beyond helping individuals and communities to "adjust," although the welfare state did remain as a safety net for the worst affected. The problems of the country were seen as unfortunate for those affected but not likely to have much impact on the rest of Australia. The agents of neo-liberalism cut the country loose from the city and left it to fend for itself.

In the late 1990s the country started to regain some political space, as an electoral backlash forced rural issues back onto the mainstream agenda. Pauline Hanson's One Nation Party was a magnet for rural grievance and destabilised many country electorates. The party was formed in 1997, after Hanson won national notoriety for her outspoken criticism of Aboriginal welfare as an endorsed Liberal during the 1996 election campaign. Then came her electrifying maiden speech, in which she attacked just about every policy assumption of the previous thirteen years of Labor government: multiculturalism, indigenous welfare, economic rationalism. City-based commentators focused on her attitudes to race and saw her as the personification of provincial ignorance and bigotry, but she was also an economic nationalist who believed the government should restore protection for manufacturing and services to the country. She spoke from the nation-building assumptions of a previous era and many country people rallied to her party. Whether they agreed with her policies or not, they were grateful to her for drawing attention back to the country. Said one rural voter, "Pauline Hanson's One Nation raised the politicians' awareness of the rural areas. All of a sudden the rest of them are showing more interest than they did before Pauline. So we have a lot to thank her for."

At the 1998 Queensland state elections One Nation won 22 per cent of the vote and eleven of the eighty-nine seats, and at the federal elections in the same year 9 per cent of the vote. Those who voted for it tended to be poorly educated, blue-collar men over fifty who lived in rural electorates, though like all parties it drew support from other demographics as well. One Nation soon imploded from its political inexperience and the contradictions of its populist promise that its parliamentarians would not be as other politicians, but it did send a wake-up call to Canberra about the deep disaffection in the country, as did the unexpected defeat of Jeff Kennett's Victorian Liberal government a year later. Kennett lost a swag of regional seats and failed to win a majority, with three rural independents holding the balance of power. In a scenario to be repeated federally in 2010, the independents chose Labor, which promised to restore services to rural Victoria. It helped, too, that the incoming premier, Steve Bracks, was from the regional town of Ballarat, in contrast to Kennett, whose enthusiasm for city-based major events had made him seem more like the premier for Melbourne than for Victoria.

In 1998, after considerable pressure from the National Party and the surge of rural voters to One Nation, the government agreed to an inquiry into the impact of the National Competition Policy reforms on the country. The resulting report shows the administrators of the neoliberal state arguing with a confused and very angry rural Australia, which still believes that the state can and should protect its prosperity and way of life. Over and over the report stresses the government's limited capacity to solve the problems of the country: "Broad long-term economic forces which are beyond the control or influence of governments have been the key drivers of economic and social changes of particular relevance to country Australia." The report's authors see government's main role as providing a broad context in which enterprises can flourish: macro-economic conditions, such as low interest rates and inflation, and a legal framework which encourages competition. In some cases, where individuals and communities are particularly adversely affected, the report does recommend that "adjustment" measures be offered. But it is wary: implementation will be difficult and government action must in no way hinder the economic processes causing the changes. Social goals were still a long way behind and rural anger was left with plenty to dwell on. A decade later, it was again the failure to focus sufficiently on social impacts that led to the mass burnings of the Murray-Darling Basin Authority's draft plan.

In 1999 the Commonwealth held a summit to discuss rural issues, and governments at all levels started to talk about "sustainability." Partnerships and grants were established to encourage regional economic development.

In getting the problems of the country back on the agenda, sustainability was a useful bridging word, linking neoliberalism's commitment to self-reliance with concerns about long-term social and environmental survival. The words "sustainable" and "regional" soon became almost inseparable, often joined by "development," as in the annual conference on Sustainable Economic Growth for Regional Australia, or the CSIRO's major research theme to support sustainable regional development. And so on. By 2000, sustainability, which had begun as an environmental concept, had expanded to include economic and social dimensions in an approach which at least recognised that there was a crisis in rural Australia. The salience of rural issues at the last election, and the government's commitment to an expensive national broadband scheme, shows that regional Australia is continuing to hold political attention.

But will Australia's regions ever be sustainable? Sustainability still carries within it the ideal that the country should stand on its own, without subsidies, or at least not too much in the way of them. The nation needs to confront the possibility that rural and regional Australia might always need a fair degree of subsidisation, that it will always be more expensive to deliver services to many parts of Australia than to the city, that we do all live in a big country with a difficult geography, and that we do all need to share the cost.

If non-metropolitan Australia is always going to need some degree of subsidy, then it needs to be underpinned by a renewed understanding of the benefits the city gets from the country. Otherwise it simply becomes a form of welfare, smoothing the dying pillow of a few old-timers in obsolete country towns and helping people leave the land through adjustment schemes. And that is no good for anyone. People in the regions have been forced to think hard about how they can build a future for themselves, as have people still engaged in agriculture. But this is not just a sectional problem, a problem for those outside the city; it is a national problem. So I want to end this essay with a stocktake. What benefits does the city get from the country?

Agriculture is still important, of course. Last year it earned about 11 per cent of Australia's export income, though it was only around 4 per cent of GDP. The National Farmers' Federation builds in a multiplier effect to claim that farms and closely related sectors comprise 12 per cent of GDP and 17 per cent of the national workforce. More importantly, however, the country feeds us, providing around 93 per cent of our daily food. Even in a nation like Australia, where few have ever experienced real hunger, this very basic level of dependence on farmers for our daily bread is psychologically powerful. A 2009 ANU poll found surprisingly high levels of sympathy for farmers, with pretty well everyone agreeing that both agriculture and rural areas were very important or fairly important to Australia's future, and a clear majority supporting assistance for agriculture (just as, come drought or flood, the media and the public continue to expect the government to provide suffering rural areas with relief). Only 3 per cent of people thought that farmers should receive less or much less assistance. One can dismiss this as some sort of agrarian hangover, or rather see it as strong recognition that even in this globalised world Australia should be able to feed itself.

The city also needs the country for pleasure and for recreation, as sea-changers, tree-changers and hobby farmers attest, as well as holiday-makers and tourists. According to the Australian regional tourism network, almost half of every tourist dollar spent here is spent outside the capital cities, with tourism employing more Australians than mining and more than forestry, agriculture and fishing combined. The spectacular development of tourism over the past few decades, both domestic and foreign, has not yet run its course. There is potential for growth in eco-tourism, and China promises a bonanza. Austrade's chief economist, Tim Harcourt, predicts that within a decade China will play the role that Japan once did as a major source of inbound tourists.

As well, despite the confidence of Australian cities in their global sophistication, the country has proved surprisingly durable when it comes to our sense of national identity. In the 1980s, as local brands like Fosters went global and we touted for international tourists, rural imagery gained new impetus. Australia now needed to represent its national distinctiveness not just to itself and the British, but also to the world at large. The colonial past, the myths of the outback and the beauties of Australia's distinctive natural environment provided the images for these marketing campaigns. The cross-over of Paul Hogan from star of 1986's *Crocodile Dundee* to tourism spruiker tells the story. Baz Luhrmann's 2008 film *Australia* worked with the same cultural palette. The 1980s also saw the development for the first time of a form of Australian national dress in the stockman's Driza-Bone and Akubra. After Howard's victory in 1996 Akubras became de rigueur for Coalition politicians: Nationals wore them pretty well all the time, and Liberals when they were in the country or at outer-suburban barbecues. The new national dress was on full display at the opening of the 2000 Olympics, which began with a riding display of Australian stock horses to the theme music of *The Man from Snowy River*. And at the 2007 APEC conference in Sydney, world leaders donned Driza-Bones for the final line-up photo.

This revival of classic outback themes and imagery is not simply a phenomenon of global marketing. Recent research by sociologists Tim Philips and Philip Smith found that the traditions of the Australian Legend were still powerful among ordinary people. Australianness was associated with the country, sport, the great outdoors, mateship, easygoing informality, voluntary associations like the Country Fire Association and surf life-saving clubs, natural icons like Ayers Rock (sic) and the Great Barrier Reef, and Australian plants and animals. For the purposes of this essay, what is interesting is the absence of urban imagery and urban experience in people's ideas about Australia. Despite the increased confidence of Australian cities, when many people try to answer for themselves the question of what it is that makes Australia distinctive, the country still supplies much of the answer.

Then there is space, room to move. By far the greatest contributor to Australia's GDP is services, at almost 50 per cent, and many of these can be provided equally well in the regions as in the cities. This is why the rural independents are so enthusiastic about the national broadband roll-out, which promises that the larger regional towns might become bigger providers of financial, design, educational and legal services. There is still a question of scale and whether regional centres can replicate the buzz from the promiscuous mix of people and ideas found in cities. But regions and towns close to the capitals are already prospering, as house prices and traffic drive people out. The new premier of New South Wales, Barry O'Farrell, is looking to decentralisation and regional development to spread New South Wales's growth beyond Sydney. It's been tried before with only marginal success, but that is no reason why it should not be tried again in the era of the internet and social networking.

The big question, however, is the land itself. This is the really difficult question: what are we to do with the continent, most of which is pretty well uninhabited? Here, you will recall, is how Katter put the problem to Leigh Sales: "I mean, if you drop a series of hydrogen bombs from the back of Cairns, the other side of Mareeba, 30 kilometres from Cairns, all the way across to Broome, you won't kill anybody. There's nobody living there ... There's only 670,000 people living on 95 per cent of the surface area of the country."

Territory is the basis of national sovereignty and it brings with it the idea that the territory should be inhabited. This, as much as the ideal of independent farming families, is what drove much of the settlement of Australia: we were a nation for a continent and thus we needed to inhabit the vast territory that we call Australia. Now that we have realised just how uninhabitable much of the country is, how are we to do this? Who is to be responsible for the land? Who is to look after it? We can't just turn our backs on the dry inland, leaving it to Mad Max, Bradley Murdoch and hordes of feral animals.

Sparseness of population does not mean, of course, that all this country is uninhabited. Much is under various forms of indigenous land owner-ship, and any new comprehensive compact between city and country must include indigenous owners. Indigenous land ownership raises large questions of historical justice as well as the complex challenges faced by many remote communities in establishing satisfying lives for themselves. A degree of subsidisation is inevitable here too, but the arguments for it are different, as are the pitfalls. However, as we think about the future of the land and how it is to be inhabited, we need to include indigenous Australians in the debate and in the solutions. Almost 70 per cent of Australia's indigenous population live in non-metropolitan areas, and, although indigenous Australians comprise only 2.2 per cent of the national population, they are increasing faster than the rest of the population. Across much of the land area, they are the dominant population. Noel Pearson's goal of an economic base for indigenous Australian communities is crucial here.

Farmers and pastoralists also inhabit much land. According to the National Farmers' Federation, farmers occupy 61 per cent of the Australian landmass, although much of this is under various forms of pastoral lease. They look after the place, and in more remote areas are important just for being there, spotting fires, noticing who is driving through, helping people who break down, and so on. Since the 1970s land-management practices have been changing to take more account of the fragile Australian environment. Much of this is motivated by resource protection, and it is inspiring innovative farmers and pastoralists to explore new ways of growing and grazing in Australian conditions. At Easter I cooked a leg of Saltbush lamb; grazed on the native vegetation of the inland, its production required no clearing and no irrigation. Also starting to take hold is the idea that farmers should be paid for ecological services. Stewardship programs in the US and Europe provide some farmers with direct payment for environmental services, such as maintaining catchment areas or taking marginal land out of production. Australia lags well behind the US and Europe in this. An estimate by Geoff Cockfield of what he calls agri-environment spending found that in 2005 per farm hectare, the UK spent US$25.10, the US $9.70 and Australia $0.1. Per farm this was UK $1514, US $2177 and Australia $453.

The difference is striking. In part it is explained by the diversion of production subsidies to ecological services when the World Trade Organization restricted the former. But it is also the case that in the northern hemisphere it has been much easier for farming practices to adapt to the new environmentalism, as there is not the fundamental ecological contradiction between farming and the natural environment that pertains to Australia. The schemes here have mostly been targeted grants for the protection of particular eco-systems, such as box-gum forests or a threatened wetland. In Australia many farmers still see environmentalism as an ill-informed, city-based movement, intruding on their turf. Similarly, the National Party has shown little interest in promoting environmental stewardship as a way of supplementing farmers' incomes. Nor has it embraced the opportunities offered by global warming and a price on carbon, focusing on increased costs to farmers rather than on potential carbon mitigation services. Not all farmers subscribe to the zombie environmental politics of the Nationals, and there are plenty of examples of environmentally innovative farmers. For example, Landcare, which began in 1989, has been a huge popular success in many rural areas, encouraging integrated, community-based approaches to environmental degradation. Nevertheless, it is clear that we need a new kind of politics that brings city environmentalists together with those who inhabit and work so much of the land, so that city and country can work together to find solutions.

Australians have largely left conservation programs to the public purse, relying on governments to save the bush as it once relied on them to settle it. There is now an extensive system of national parks, which is being gradually added to. But, as species are lost and ecosystems decline, some Australians are no longer relying on government action. In 1991 Martin Copley founded Australian Wildlife Conservancy, purchasing land to establish sanctuaries for threatened species and protect vulnerable ecosystems. Another private not-for-profit organisation, the Victorian Trust for Nature, purchases properties and works with landholders to conserve native bushland. These are small, given the size of the territory, but they add another form of land management to the already existing mosaic.

This stocktake is partial: there are other ways in which the city needs and relies on the people and the land beyond the urban areas. But let me close on the larger point: there has been so much attention paid in the past few decades to the *problems* of the country, both from the country itself and from city-based commentators. What we need now is to rebalance the debate and focus on the strengths of the country and on its potential. There are the obligations of citizenship here, to bridge the gap with indigenous Australians and to maintain as much as possible equality of essential services for the 30 per cent of us living in rural and regional areas. And there are obligations of nationhood. We are a nation for a large and varied continent and we need to rediscover the sense of obligation possessed by our federation forebears, who believed they had to make good the claim and inhabit and use the land. So should we.

SOURCES

The arguments and ideas in the essay had a first run in an article, "The Country, the City and the State," published in 2007 in *The Australian Journal of Political Science*, Vol. 42, No. 1, pp. 1–17. Watching the fall-out of the 2010 election I thought it worth expanding them for a broader audience.

General Sources

Bill Pritchard and Phil McManus (eds), *Land of Discontent: The Dynamics of Change in Rural Australia*, UNSW Press, Sydney, 2000.
Stewart Lockie and Lisa Bourke (eds), *Rurality Bites: The Social and Environmental Transformation of Rural Australia*, Pluto Press, Annandale NSW, 2001.
Chris Cocklin and Jacqui Diblin (eds), *Sustainability and Change in Rural Australia*, UNSW Press, Sydney, 2005.
Linda Botterill and Geoff Cockfield (eds), *The National Party: Prospects for the Great Survivor*, Allen & Unwin, Sydney, 2009.

2   "'a debate that's been politically marketed into Western Sydney ...'": Tony Windsor and Bob Katter were interviewed by Leigh Sales on ABC *Lateline*, "Independents could decide the nation's future," 16 August 2010.

3   "long history of the rivalry between the Country and the City ...": Raymond Williams, *The Country and the City*, Chatto & Windus, London, 1973.

5   "The clincher was Labor's commitment to broadband ...": "Broadband the key in Rob Oakeshott and Tony Windsor's decision to back Gillard," *Courier Mail*, 8 September 2010.

7   "John Howard also evoked it in his projection of himself as an ordinary Australian bloke ...": see Judith Brett, *Quarterly Essay 19, Relaxed & Comfortable: The Liberal Party's Australia*, Black Inc., Melbourne, August 2005.

7   "as she fights off accusations from other premiers that Tasmania has become a mendicant ...": Lara Giddings was cited in "Clean, green and leaning on the mainland," *The Australian*, 9 April 2011.

9   "said the plan was devastating for his community ...": Adrian Piccoli was cited in "Anger spills over at water cuts meeting," ABC *Riverina*, 14 October 2010.

11   "'I've watched friends of mine commit suicide ...'": "Kingmaker Katter kicks into Canberra," *Sydney Morning Herald*, 24 August 2010.

12   "A convention in Armidale in 1921 attracted 220 delegates from 124 New State leagues ...": Figures from Ulrich Ellis, *The Country Party: A Political and Social History of the Party in New South Wales*, F.W. Cheshire, Melbourne, 1958, pp. 83, 138.

12   "the tensions of the Depression were displaced onto the eastern states ...":
      Geoffrey Bolton, *A Fine Country to Starve in*, UWA Press/Edith Cowan University,
      Nedlands, WA, 1994.

13   "'the secession sentiment is alive and well ...'": Sir Richard Court's address
      can be found in the *Proceedings of the Samuel Griffith Society*, Vol. 3, available at
      http://samuelgriffith.org.au/docs/vol3/Vol3.pdf.

13   "The Liberal premier, Colin Barnett, is fighting federal Labor ...": "Canberra
      doesn't understand the West," *The Australian*, 2 December 2010.

13   "'We can accept that we share this prosperity ...'": Colin Barnett was cited in
      "Mining blows up fair go federalism," *The Weekend Australian*, 2–3 April 2011.

14   "Western Australia will secede by stealth ...": "'Beggar' state drains GST says
      Barnett," *The Australian*, 4 April 2011.

14   "Labor was well ahead in Victoria on the two-party-preferred ...": "Coalition
      surges to decisive lead," *The Age*, 14 February 2011.

20   "36 per cent of the population of New South Wales lived in Sydney ...": Figures
      from J.M. Powell, *An Historical Geography of Modern Australia: The Restive Fringe*, Cam-
      bridge University Press, Cambridge, 1988, pp. 23, 31.

20   "rural areas had higher fertility rates ...": Graeme Davison, "Rural Sustainability
      in Historical Perspective," in Cocklin and Dibden (eds), p. 47.

22   "'We shall be ensuring that the number of voters in each electorate is much
      closer than it is now to the ideal of equality ...'" Whitlam gave the opening
      speech at the Joint Sitting of Parliament, 6 August 1974.

22   "During the 1980s, as Queensland's population swelled ...": Ross Fitzgerald et
      al., *Made in Queensland: A New History*, UQP, St Lucia, 2009, p. 180.

23   "People in the bush want the NBN ...": "Pipe dreams," *The Age*, 19 February
      2011, p. 17.

24   "In 1999 the two recipients, Tasmania and the Northern Territory ...": Produc-
      tivity Commission, *Impact of Competition Policy Reform on Rural and Regional Australia*,
      Inquiry Report, No. 8, 1999, p. 18.

26   "in the settler societies of Australia, the US, Canada, Argentina and New Zealand
      ...": Boris Schedvin, "The Australian Economy on the hinge of history," *Austral-
      ian Economic Review*, Vol. 20, No. 1, 1987, pp. 20–30.

27   "putting a man on the land 'provides a job for one man and probably two men
      in the city ...'": Hughes was cited in Colin Forster, *Industrial Development in Australia
      1920–1930*, ANU Press, Canberra, 1964, p. 171.

28   "'Australia's aim above everything else is to populate her country and advance
      from her position ...'" Bruce was cited in Sean Glynn, *Government Policy and Agri-
      cultural Development*, UWA Press, Nedlands, WA, 1975, p. 73.

29   "it was also paid in the hard work and heartbreak of the many men and women ...": Stuart Macintyre, *The Oxford History of Australia 1901–1942*, Vol. 4, Oxford University Press, Melbourne, 1986, pp. 200–10.

30   "As the historian Keith Hancock observed...": *Australia*, Benn, London, 1930, p. 71.

30   "'All of these things were within the authority of the government ...'": *John McEwen: His Story*, privately printed, 1983.

31   "'Without such a policy Australia will cease to be a nation ...'": cited in Alan Davies and Geoffrey Serle (eds), *Policies for Progress: Essays in Australian Politics*, Cheshire, Melbourne, p. 154.

32   "'The aggregation of cities is like a wen ...'": *The Leader*'s warning was cited in Graeme Davison, "Rural Sustainability in Historical Perspective," in Cocklin and Dibden (eds), p. 47.

32   "'I hope I'm not being parochial ...'": cited in Judith Brett and Anthony Moran, *Ordinary People's Politics: Australians Talk about Life, Politics and the Future of Their Country*, Pluto Press, North Melbourne, 2006, p. 21.

33   "Russel Ward summed this up in 1958 ...": for a summary of Ward's influential argument and discussion of the Australian Legend, see the entry "The Australian Legend" by Michael Roe in Gwenda Beed Davey and Graham Seal (eds), *The Oxford Companion to Australian Folklore*, Oxford University Press, Melbourne, 1993.

34   "John Hirst argues that the Australian Legend has a rival rural legend ...": "The Pioneer Legend," *Historical Studies*, Vol. 18, No. 71, 1978, pp. 316–37.

34   "coined the term 'countrymindedness' to describe the worldview of country Australia ...": Don Aitkin, "Countrymindedness – the spread of an idea," in Samuel Goldberg and Francis Smith (eds), *Australian Cultural History*, Cambridge University Press, Cambridge, 1988, p. 51.

36   "Whereas primary products had made up two-thirds of world trade ...": figures from Hugh Emy and Owen Hughes, *Australian Politics: Realities in Conflict*, second edition, Macmillan, South Melbourne, 1988.

36   "By 1970 wool, which had provided 47 per cent of Australia's export income ...": "The wool industry – looking back and forward," *Australian Yearbook 2003*, Australian Bureau of Statistics, 1301.1.

37   "corporate farms account for an increasing acreage ..." Matthew Tonts and Alan Black, *The Impact of Changing Farm Business Structures on Rural Communities*, Report for the Rural Industries research Development Corporation, No. 02/027, 2001.

39   "Between 1947 and 1996 the proportion of the rural population born overseas increased ...": Graeme Hugo, "Regional Australia: Definitions, Diversity and

Dichotomy," paper presented to the Social Policy Research Centre, UNSW, June 2001, pp. 16–19; Antony Green, "Bush Politics," in Lockie and Bourke (eds), p. 69.

40 "Hegemonic masculinity has persisted ...": see Margaret Alston, "Gender Perpectives in Australian Rural Community Life," in Cocklin and Dibden (eds), p. 139.

42 "'We feel that we are at the end of the line, forgotten ...'": Jennifer Curtin, *The Voice and Vote of the Bush: The Representation of Rural and Regional Australia in the Federal Parliament*, Department of Parliamentary Services, Parliamentary Library, Commonwealth of Australia, 2004.

44 "My early farm experience formed the basis of a lot of my views ...": *John McEwen: His Story*.

45 "thirty-three balding Anglo men, with diversity provided by a few Catholics and Doug Anthony's full head of hair ...": photo, Paul Davey, *Ninety Not Out: The Nationals 1920–2010*, UNSW Press, Sydney, 2010, p. 168.

46 "In the 1970s the Country Party had averaged around 10 per cent of the federal vote ...": figures taken from http://elections.uwa.edu.au.

49 "A key aim of agricultural policy became to encourage owners of unviable farms to 'exit the industry ...'": Darren Halpin, "The collective political action of the Australian farming and rural communities: putting farm interest groups in context," *Rural Society*, Vol. 13, No. 2, pp. 138–57.

49 "in 1992 the National Drought Policy redefined drought ...": Linda Courtenay Botterill and Donald A. Wilhite (eds), *From Disaster Response to Risk Management: Australia's National Drought Policy*, Springer, Dordrecht, The Netherlands, 2005.

50 "following corporatisation, Australia Post reduced the numbers of post offices ...": Rolf Gerritsen, *Deregulating Australia Post: Another Attack on Regional Australia*, ACRLGS Monographs on Applied Policy, No. 1, University of Canberra, Canberra, 1998.

51 "Treasuries and finance departments, intent on balancing budgets and producing surpluses ...": Rolf Gerritson, "The management of government and its consequences for service delivery in Regional Australia," in Pritchard and McManus (eds).

51 "Jennifer Curtin, who talked with rural voters in the early 2000s ...": *The Voice and Vote of the Bush*.

52 "'The sense of alienation, of being left behind ...'": John Anderson, "One Nation or Two?", Address to the National Press Club, 1999.

52 "Fischer told the rural NSW paper *The Land* that he was 'fed up with people saying the Government is doing nothing ...'": "What rural crisis?" *The Land*, 10 July 1997.

54   "'Pauline Hanson's One Nation raised the politicians' awareness of the rural areas ...'": Curtin, p. 23.

54   "Those who voted for it tended to be poorly educated, blue-collar men over fifty who lived in rural electorates ...": Clive Bean, "Nationwide electoral support for One Nation," in Michael Leach et al. (eds), *The Rise and Fall of One Nation*, UQP, St Lucia, Qld, 2000.

55   "the government agreed to an inquiry into the impact of the National Competition Policy reforms on the country ...": John Anderson, "One Nation or Two?", Address to the National Press Club, 1999; Productivity Commission, *Impact of Competition Policy Reform on Rural and Regional Australia*.

55   "the key drivers of economic and social changes of particular relevance to country Australia ...": Productivity Commission, Summary Finding 8, XLIV.

57   "A 2009 ANU poll found surprisingly high levels of sympathy for farmers ...": Geoff Cockfield and Linda Botterill, "Testing agrarian myths: attitudes to Australian agriculture," paper presented to the Australian Political Studies Association Conference, 2010.

58   "Recent research by sociologists ...": Tim Phillips and Philip Smith, "What is Australian? Knowledge and attitudes among a gallery of contemporary Australians," *Australian Journal of Political Science*, Vol. 35, No. 2, 2000, pp. 223–4.

60   "Almost 70 per cent of Australia's indigenous population live in non-metropolitan areas ...": Graeme Hugo, "The state of rural populations," in Cocklin and Dibden (eds).

60   "An estimate by Geoff Cockfield of what he calls agri-environment spending ...": figures from Botterill and Cockfield, p. 133.

Robert Dessaix

What an unruly grab-bag of a word "happiness" is, an *omnium gatherum* of dove-tailing concepts from "contentment" to "joy." With reassuring elegance and just the right amount of erudition to impress but not intimidate his readers, David Malouf has tried to bring a little order to the chaos. Although I am not sure that he has distilled the essence of what we mean (or Europeans in particular have meant across the centuries) either by "happiness" or "the happy life," he stimulated me at every point, as a good essayist does, to ask myself awkward questions about my own accustomed thoughts on "happiness" – my own approach to leading "the happy life." I'd have liked to come across a uniquely Maloufian twist to arguments about what happiness is, rather than a tapestry of others' thoughts, but that is to quibble. The tapestry is finely woven.

What really interests Malouf, he tells us, is not how to live if we want to be happy, but why happiness still eludes so many of us now that the "chief sources of human unhappiness … have largely been removed from our lives." As I understand it, Malouf believes that it has something to do with realising at last that we are alone in an infinite void, the playthings of something capricious called the Economy (which nobody understands), unable to feel at home anywhere, attached only to surfaces. I was not convinced by this argument: it sounds plausible as an explanation of contemporary Western unease (if there is widespread unease), but Malouf supplies no evidence to suggest that this is in fact what is making modern Westerners unhappy (if that's what they are). A lot of them certainly look bored.

Thinkers from other traditions might just as plausibly argue that we are still unhappy, despite our freedom from the miseries afflicting medieval man, because we are still chained to desire – indeed, inflaming desires of various kinds is the very engine of the modern Western economy. Or perhaps the Prometheus story, so illuminatingly discussed by Malouf, gives us the key: unrest is simply part and parcel of being human – or, in modern terms, a capacity for dissatisfaction makes humankind the inventive, technologically skilled species it needs to be to survive and evolve.

Happy moments are not so difficult to come by for most of us, as Malouf points out. Small surges of pleasure mark most of our days – and not only in advanced economies – and for each of us their sources will be different. Some will be exhilarated by a visit to Harvey Norman, some seized by joy at a performance of *La Traviata* or *Hairspray*, others at peace with themselves stroking the dog in front of the fire, content after a day in the garden, deeply satisfied by a good book or ecstatic at the prospect of erotic fulfilment. Yet none of those things makes any of us truly happy people. And there's the rub: pleasurable moments (like Ivan Denisovich's when he looked back over his "undarkened" day) do not make us happy people. It is being profoundly, rootedly happy – living a happy life – as opposed to merely content or fleetingly euphoric, that presents more of a problem. For that sort of happiness some other kind of awareness, underlying all our days, is needed.

It is easy, I think, in considering what this sort of awareness might be, to mistake the starting points for achieving it for the thing itself. For some the starting point might be solitude in Montaigne's "little back-shop," for others tumult, for some oneness with the godhead. It depends on your circumstances. It is true that, historically, in the English (and German and Russian) words for "happiness" two areas of meaning dovetailed: "luck" and "pleasure," giving us a meaning Malouf nicely sums up as "the state of being in good standing in the world of accident and event … pleased with what life has brought you." This kind of basic satisfaction with your place in the world, while seemingly at odds with the Promethean idea, may be a good point of departure for pursuing a happy life, but not much more.

That is why the line that Malouf quotes from *One Day in the Life of Ivan Denisovich* ("The day had gone by without a single cloud – almost a happy day.") strikes me as an unsatisfactory climax to his ruminations on happiness. Malouf interprets this line about Shukhov's "almost happy day" in the labour camp as an affirmation of the possibility of happiness "within limits." Accommodating yourself to what your world makes possible is a good place to start, but it cannot be the goal of any "search for contentment" of a lasting kind. In any case, in the original Russian Shukhov simply has a moment of "satisfaction," reflecting back on a day that has passed, a day described as "undarkened by anything" (not "cloudless," which implies brightness), "almost happy" – that is to say, free of added miseries – not as actually "happy." In fact, I would be tempted to translate "*pochti schastlivy den*'" as "almost a fortunate day" rather than "happy."

Whatever the prelude to a happy life – rest, rebellion, satisfaction, unease – it seems to me that what characterises lasting happiness is a feeling of freedom. "The little back-shop, all our own, entirely free," Montaigne wrote. And I think he hit the nail on the head. Whether or not freedom is an illusion is unimportant – perhaps indeed we are no freer than cabbages to choose how we might grow. But unlike cabbages we can *feel* free – and happiness is a feeling.

As I see it, what is vital is not what we free ourselves from (that will always depend on our individual circumstances), but what we free ourselves to do. Ultimately, I believe that happiness results from freeing ourselves to magnify our sense of our humanity – to be more intensely, consciously, inventively, adventurously human ("ourselves," if you like) – and to take pleasure in what grows out of this. When we hear people say that they're happy when they're at a heavy metal concert or stoned or talking to Jesus or living in a Tuscan village or alone at home with the cat, reading a good book, I think they're really telling us about an inkling they've had of what happiness is for them, about a step towards it, a beginning they've made in its pursuit, not about happiness itself. The freedom you need to be deeply, abidingly happy requires a self-knowledge, I would say even a virtuosity, that few have possessed in any era. As André Gide wrote, to free yourself is nothing – it's being free that's hard.

Robert Dessaix

Anne Manne

In Ovid's hauntingly beautiful poem *Metamorphoses*, he tells of a prophecy given by the blind seer Tiresias on the birth of Narcissus: "If he but fail to recognise himself, a long life he may have, beneath the sun."

Narcissus grows into a young man celebrated and desired for his beauty, yet he spurns and humiliates all who court him. One of his would-be lovers, the nymph Echo, follows him everywhere but is brutally repelled. Rejected, "hiding her blushing face", "her great love increases with neglect; her miserable body wastes away, wakeful with sorrows," until nothing "remains except her voice that lives, that lives among the hills."

Nemesis, the much-feared Goddess of Divine Retribution, is angered by the cruelty of Narcissus. She is the restorer of the proper order of things, who punishes arrogance, hubris, those who commit crimes with impunity.

Drinking at a mountain pool, Narcissus becomes enchanted by the beauty of his own image reflected in the water. "All that is lovely in himself he loves, and in his witless way he wants himself: he who approves is equally approved; he seeks, is sought, he burns and he is burnt." "Crazed with love," Narcissus cannot bear to disturb the lily pond carrying his beloved image. He pines away and dies of thirst. All that remains of the beautiful youth is a white flower, narcissus.

In *The Happy Life*, David Malouf interrogates the strange disparity between our conquering the material conditions of life and our state of restless discontent, and asks why contentment – happiness – seems to have eluded us. There is much to admire in the essay and the gentle spirit with which it unfolds, echoing, one guesses, the quiet contentment of its author. His perceptions are characteristically delicate. The sources he uses are satisfyingly deep and the insights fresh.

So beguiling is the style that it seems almost churlish to complain. Yet object

I must. For Malouf's perceptions remain disparate, and the argument, for all its grace of expression, remains imprecise and diffuse. Consequently we are left with tantalising fragments of insight where we might hope for a denouement.

Although Malouf intuits many of the surface aspects of our contemporary discontents, he fails to get at the culture underpinning our malaise, nor its psychological architecture. So where might we find a coherent conceptual framework to make sense of the fragmentary insights of Malouf's beautifully written but ultimately unsatisfying sketch?

Strangely, it is right there in the classical source to which Malouf turns. He discusses Ovid's poem, but misses entirely the depiction of the crucial myth of Narcissus and the light it might throw on our contemporary malaise. The underlying problem impeding our "pursuit of happiness," undermining our "search for contentment," lies in the contemporary culture of narcissism.

Language matters. It is no surprise that so fine a novelist as Malouf has an acute ear for tones, textures and meanings embedded in language. He turns to classical sources, including the Greeks, to illuminate our search for happiness. And indeed the Greek word *eudemonia*, roughly translated, means happiness. But, as Wittgenstein warned, we need to be attentive to how language "relates to a way of living" and is embedded in "the kinds of lives and practices" from which it derives. Hence it cannot be extracted from "the activities into which it is woven" without loss of meaning. To remove a word from its cultural context is like hearing only the top melodic note in a chord of music. The top note might be happiness, thinly interpreted, but the richer full chord of *eudemonia* resonates with intimations of the virtues: courage, justice, moderation, discipline and an examined life. A life like Socrates', who was willing to swallow hemlock and die, for truth is worth dying for. Or, as Plato suggested, the good life is one in which it is better to suffer evil than to do it. For the Greeks, then, *eudemonia* sounds these deeper notes, where the happiness of human flourishing is inextricably tied to the life-practice of the virtues.

Some of the loveliest passages in the essay are in his analysis of the paintings by Rembrandt and Rubens and the famous love poem by Donne. Malouf's sensitive account shows the kind of happiness possible when sensuality and love are united, and undistorted by Christian bodily shame. The attractiveness of these passages comes from the fact that each of the works centres on a sexual intimacy in which the Other is fully, joyously present, as love and desire moves toward them and is returned. The glorying is not in the Self but in the Other. There is such ease in their faces! Trust makes the self-forgetfulness which liberates Eros possible. The space between two people is utterly alive. Malouf juxtaposes the visions of happiness depicted there – lush, erotic, joyous – against the dour, shame-ridden sexual repression of Christianity.

Yet this looking backwards, at another era, as opposed to examining our own world, obscures the fact that we face quite different problems. In analysing our time, Malouf would have done better to examine the powerful, haunting painting of Narcissus by Caravaggio. There is no Other. A solitary figure is illuminated against a dark backdrop and stares with such intensity and desire at his own image that all else ceases to exist, falls away into darkness, obliterated from sight. There is only Narcissus and the pool on which his lonely image floats.

For the kind of relatedness that Malouf celebrates as being at the centre of human happiness is precisely our weakest point, where our hopes are most distant from our desires. We have record numbers of family breakdowns, commitment phobia, the rise of loneliness and its dark companions, depression, anxiety and even suicide. There is a tendency for the deepest human relationships to be commodified and to have meaning emptied from them. If happiness is about anything, surely it is about meaning, and in the wake of these changes there has been for too many a collapse of just that, with all the anxiety and anguish that come with postmodernity's unbearable lightness of being.

The historian Eric Hobsbawm has argued that by the end of the '60s there had occurred "a triumph of the individual over society", a "self-regarding individualism pushed to its limits ... The world was now tacitly assumed to consist of several billion human beings defined by their pursuit of individual desire."

That too, said differently, is the conclusion of a leading contemporary psychoanalyst, Peter Fonagy. "In recent years," he remarks, "issues of narcissism have taken centre-stage." It is always important to understand in a thinker what they are moving against. Malouf seems much more alive to the barrier to happiness as it was in Freud's time, when the central problem was sexual repression. Yet the hysterias born of sexual inhibition have long since given way to quite different problems, disorders of the self such as narcissism. Love is turned inward; for all too many there is no Other.

Narcissism is characterised by an overweening sense of entitlement, exploitativeness, hyper-competitiveness, lack of empathy, vicious rage when thwarted, inability to love or maintain relationships, and grandiosity, a sense of superiority born of our "specialness" which entitles us to privileges. Whatever is good for the self is good. It is self-destructive and destructive of others, just as in the myth of Narcissus.

Christopher Lasch first wrote his book *The Culture of Narcissism* in 1979, yet the problem has grown much, much worse since then. By the time Jean Twenge and

W. Keith Campbell wrote their 2009 book *The Narcissism Epidemic*, many of Lasch's examples looked tame. And the problem is now more widespread. Measures of narcissism show it to be steadily rising amongst college populations with every succeeding generation. The title of a book penned by a TV *Bachelorette* star reads *Better Single than Sorry: A No-Regrets Guide to Loving Yourself and Never Settling*. Even evangelical Christians accept the premise. "Love God, love yourself, love others, in that order," advised one megachurch pastor.

So many contemporary problems derive from narcissism. The ugly sense of entitlement and lack of empathy are evident in all forms of bullying, road rage and flaming in the blogosphere. These are not only examples of incivility, but also of narcissistic rage. A recent analysis of hit songs shows how songs once lamented the loss of a beloved, but now brag of physical prowess or make aggressive sexual demands.

There is a link too, that Malouf misses, between the brave new world of the "permanent temporariness of relationships," as sociologist Zygmunt Bauman describes it, and the "body project." The fleeting "hook-up" establishes a competitive free market of bodies. The self is profoundly reshaped. The historian Joan Jacobs Brumberg found that in the late nineteenth century girls scarcely mentioned their bodies in diary entries. Moral language was reserved for improving character. In a diary of 1892, for example, there is the entry: "Resolved, not to talk about myself or my feelings. To think before speaking. To work seriously. To be self-restrained in conversation and action. Not to let my thoughts wander. To be dignified. Interest myself more in others." But a diary entry in 1982 shows that the cult of self-improvement now resides in the body: "I will try to make myself better in any way I possibly can with the help of my budget and babysitting money, I will lose weight, get new lenses, already got a new haircut, good make-up, new clothes and accessories."

Increasingly, this new "self" is delivered by plastic surgery. Malouf discusses the lovely Rubens painting, but any depiction in modern times of such a generous form would send an upper-middle-class woman scurrying for liposuction and a surgical nip and tuck. Once the strategy of ageing Hollywood stars, the numbers of such procedures have skyrocketed. As always, it is the land of the "free" which is the most extreme, but the same trends are followed elsewhere. Most importantly, the devout belief here is that a better appearance delivers not just happiness but a new self. In the ubiquitous human makeover programs, a new self emerges from the old like a butterfly from a chrysalis.

Nor should one underestimate how profoundly this "Look at Me!" sense of self has shifted because it has developed under the gaze of our peers – "the grid of 200 million," as George Frow puts it – rather than the gods. In one of the earliest twentieth-century critiques of celebrity, Billy Wilder's *Sunset Boulevard*, Gloria Swanson's character, like all narcissists, finds ageing impossible. She consoles herself with a celluloid version of the lily pond, obsessively watching her younger self perform every night. When her lover/prisoner shows interest in someone else, she shoots him. But *Sunset Boulevard* was a critique, and understood as such. Now the shift towards self-admiration means being famous is considered a kind of new *right*. Perhaps even an obligation. Youngsters in the West increasingly declare being famous as their most important goal in life. In one study, US college students felt that having high self-esteem, feeling good about oneself, was more important than any other value: good grades, friendship, love and even sex. This narcissism is given endless means of expression through reality TV and social networking.

Malouf comments on the dent to our happiness from "stress" but does not do enough to identify the causes. A narcissistic society is hyper-competitive. It is a society where, as Twenge and Campbell put it, there are "a lot of sharp elbows." In this context Malouf mentions our obedience to "the Economy," an entity too large to control. Yet our economic predicaments, global, national and individual, are hardly separate from narcissism either. It is behind the wild grandiosity of CEO salaries, the selfishness of tax cuts to the mega-rich, and the catastrophic mismanagement by Wall Street of other people's money. Equally it is implicated in the stressed individual of the straining and groaning "working family," which delivers more hours per family to service their heavy burden of debt. Like Narcissus, we are all too often in love with an illusion. When one thirst is slaked, another "need" emerges to take its place.

Towards the end of the essay, Malouf describes our concern over "the Planet" as further adding to our stress. Like "the Economy," it is too big an idea for people to cope with. There is something in this insight. Yet surely he should go further. Recall the prophetic words of Tiresias, warning that if Narcissus does not recognise who he is and what he is doing, he will perish. In the form of climate change, the Planet is presently delivering warning of retribution as if from Nemesis, the dark and dangerous goddess of balance, daughter of Justice, whose "adamantine bridles" restrain "the frivolous insolences of mortals." But like Narcissus, we go on gazing at the lily pond, enchanted and intoxicated by all that we see there, those trappings of the good life that reflect us back so much larger and more dazzling than we really are, maybe all the way to extinction.

Anne Manne

Robert Lagerberg

As a regular teacher of Solzhenitsyn's *One Day in the Life of Ivan Denisovich*, I have misgivings about David Malouf's reading of this book, particularly his conclusion: "Unlikely as it may seem, Shukhov is our perfect example of the happy man. And we understand his state, and believe him when he tells us he is happy, because we have lived through this day with him."

Shukhov is offered by Malouf as the embodiment of a type, the downtrodden person who is nonetheless able to derive a certain amount of happiness from his meagre lot, when not ravaged by more extreme pain or tragedy, and when blessed by the smallest bounties. His "happiness" is relative, and results from small mercies – surviving another day, risking but escaping solitary confinement, scraping a few extra bowls of food (if the vile swill he eats can be called that), and taking part in a productive and warming work session on the construction site, albeit in freezing conditions and wearing the most rudimentary clothing and footwear.

There are several reasons to avoid a simplistic reading of this kind. Solzhenitsyn himself never really expected his book to be published under the Soviet regime. Taking advantage of Khrushchev's 1961 criticism of Stalin, he decided, albeit nervously, to submit his manuscript to the journal *Novyj mir*. Through no small amount of luck, it finally found its way to an editor and thence to Khrushchev himself, who recommended that it be published, saying: "[I]t is a life-affirming work. In fact I'll go so far as to say that it expresses the Party spirit." Undoubtedly the book would not have been published if its hero had been portrayed as in any way subversive. Shukhov is earthy, but smart and even kind; he is a peasant and – undoubtedly deliberately – a non-intellectual in contrast to the cultivated main character of Dostoyevsky's towering work of Russian prison life, *The House of the Dead*. Shukhov survives the Gulag so well precisely because he does not ask himself the difficult questions. With its explosive subject matter, *One Day in the Life of*

Ivan Denisovich had to give a dispassionate description of the day itself, with some semblance of a positive statement at its conclusion, in order to be published.

Malouf's reading ignores this most basic form of irony – the portrayal of dire conditions without overt commentary – to claim with a straight face that the hero has found happiness … almost. The latter word is key, of course: "The day had gone by without a single cloud – *almost* a happy day." Certainly, it would be hard to reconcile the author of the astringent *Gulag Archipelago*, with its graphic descriptions of Stalin's labour camps, with the author of this "happy day." I think that Solzhenitsyn himself would have been surprised to learn that he had provided Malouf with a "perfect example of the happy man."

One should bear in mind all that is not mentioned explicitly about the camps, but which this book conjured up in the minds of its readers: the false or petty convictions, the long and arbitrary sentences, the terrifyingly awful journeys to the camps, the cruelty and death there, the appalling physical conditions – freezing winters and scorching summers with inadequate clothing and terrible food – the stench, lice, the danger from hardened criminals, particularly at night, the fate of women and even babies …

Malouf also ignores an important point made by the punctuation of the original text: the two short final paragraphs of the book are separated from the preceding material by a line break. This break between "almost a happy day" and the final paragraph signifies, in my view, one of the largest intakes of breath in the history of literature, as it precedes a vast silent scream, the visceral comprehension of hell on earth that results from the act of remembering – the other "half" of the book. Even assuming one day of relative happiness, the addition of 3652 more such days scarcely bodes well. My reading of the book is, therefore, of two very unequal "halves": the first 99.9 per cent as Shukhov slowly "awakens" to recall his day, even to acknowledge, at its close, that it was, to paraphrase, "not all that bad"; and the final 0.1 per cent, in the form of the last paragraph, when it is realised that the good fortune and almost superhuman effort required to guide him safely through this day is dwarfed in every way by the scale of ten years, or, as in the case of one of the inmates – surely one of the most moving passages of the book – who "had been in prison … as long as the Soviet state had existed … and … as soon as he finished one tenner they'd pinned another on him."

The relative happiness of Shukhov's one day is crushed by the terrifying weight of the closing paragraph, and the persisting note is one of deep despair.

Robert Lagerberg

Tim Soutphommasane

I find much of the recent writing on the topic of happiness and wellbeing rather frustrating, if not entirely disappointing. This is because so much of it is the work of economists who are interested primarily in measuring happiness. The very act of measuring happiness leads us down the wrong path. It implies that happiness exists as something we should seek to maximise. It also suggests that happiness, whether individual or societal, can be achieved as a matter of rational calculation. Our economist friends, those practitioners of the dismal science, would typically say that the key to unlocking happiness is to focus on the right variables.

David Malouf's essay is an elegant and humane corrective to such vulgar utilitarianism. As Malouf observes, the trouble with trying to measure happiness is two-fold. First, we cannot measure happiness as such but only certain proxies for it, such as income, education or health. Second, in dealing only with general and quantifiable factors, statistical representations of happiness fail to account for how happiness is singular and subjective: "It belongs to the world of what is felt, what cannot be presented or numbered on a scale because it cannot be seen." It is this very elusive quality that makes the search for contentment a perennial topic of contemplation.

I agree with Malouf that much of our discussions about happiness are in fact about the social conditions we associate with a good standard of living. I concur too with his observation that as a word happiness is so widely used that we have come to regard it as synonymous with terms like contentment and satisfaction. Adding to this, I would say that many Australians make no distinction between happiness, wellbeing and quality of life. We assume someone to be happy, and to be living well, if they enjoy a good quality of life.

To what extent, though, might greater clarity in our language contribute to a better understanding of what living well should mean? Certainly, happiness and wellbeing do not mean the same thing. The philosopher Bernard Williams wrote that while it makes sense to say that one feels happy one day, yet unhappy the next, wellbeing implicates the shape of one's whole life. Malouf's references to Alexander Solzhenitsyn's Shukhov, the "happy" Russian prisoner in *One Day in the Life of Ivan Denisovich*, indicate he shares this view; as he puts it, happiness is something that can be enjoyed only in "moments of self-fulfilment." His appeals to classical tradition, as restated by the likes of Montaigne and Sir Henry Wotton (a forgotten Renaissance man if there ever was one), suggest he believes there can be a higher form of happiness, one which is accompanied by virtue and wisdom.

Discussing matters in such terms reminds us of one thing: living well involves a life of ethical flourishing. Happiness might not be the self-evident purpose of the good life, but something derivative of wellbeing. We miss a trick in regarding happiness, wellbeing and quality of life as identical concepts. Rather, we should say that wellbeing refers to the *end* of seeking the good life; that happiness is a *symptom* of wellbeing; and that quality of life represents a composite of those social *conditions* required for flourishing.

An ethical view of happiness challenges our modern perspective. At one level, we tend to regard happiness as merely sentiment or emotion. At another, as Malouf writes, "The good life as we understand it has to do with what we call lifestyle, with living it up in a world that offers us gifts or goodies free for the taking." Current concerns about the cost of living and quality of life reveal there are serious limits to a lifestyle view of happiness: the logic of happiness-as-material lifestyle involves a sense of perpetual crisis. If the public conversation is any indication, many Australians today feel that a decent quality of life is becoming harder to attain. Many of us have higher and higher expectations of what a good life should involve, and believe we can never have it good enough. Such subjective feelings are disconnected from objective realities. Only rarely do we remember that surveys regularly indicate that Australia remains one of the best places in the world in which to live and that we have little cause for complaint. The UNDP's Human Development Index of 2010, for example, placed us second behind Norway as the most developed country in the world.

Malouf notes that much of this concern can be attributed to a restlessness, which is only becoming more acute. In an age of iPhones, Twitter and 24-hour news, it seems that constant unrest is now itself becoming a cure for our "existential state of anxiety." We could simply blame the Americans (I am only half-joking). If Thomas Jefferson and his fellow founding fathers of the republic were responsible for making the pursuit of happiness an inalienable right of mankind, then they may be just as responsible for the restlessness. In his *Democracy in America*, Alexis de Tocqueville noted the tireless striving of individuals "in the midst of abundance":

> Their taste for physical gratifications must be regarded as the original source of that secret disquietude which the actions of the Americans betray and of that inconstancy of which they daily afford fresh examples. He who has set his heart exclusively upon the pursuit of worldly welfare is always in a hurry, for he has but a limited time at his disposal to reach, to grasp, and to enjoy it. The recollection of the shortness of life is a constant spur to him. Besides the good things that he possesses, he every instant fancies a thousand others that death will prevent him from trying if he does not try them soon. This thought fills him with anxiety, fear, and regret and keeps his mind in ceaseless trepidation, which leads him perpetually to change his plans and his abode.

Any ethos of self-sufficiency finds a more natural home in the Old World than in the New World that America epitomised; yet the real question is whether our modern sensibilities are essentially fixed. This seems to be the unresolved challenge presented by *The Happy Life*. Malouf is resigned to accepting that in advanced and highly managed societies, "the good life and the happy life ... belong to separate and in some ways unconnected meanings of happy." But if there is in this a philosophical acceptance of the distinction, this may be yielding too much, too easily, to our dominant language of lifestyle. Such a concession seems to grant that the good life, properly understood, is indeed something material; and that the best we can hope for are fleeting moments of satisfaction, given that *eudemonia* and flourishing were fit only for the ancients.

Surely there is something to be said for reinstating the good life as an unambiguously ethical aspiration. A more muscular ethical view may enable us to confront the impersonality that is one of the causes of our discontent (as Malouf puts it, the fact that we "cannot put a face" to those forces of Economy that shape our lives). I do wonder what kind of Australia would exist if we could converse about wellbeing without always referring so stubbornly to lifestyle. Imagine if we could understand that the good life need not be defined so narrowly as a sanctuary of sun and surf and suburbs. Australians may then find that anxiety about their way of life, and an inability to find happiness, might have more to do with insatiable wants, unreasonable expectations and an addiction to middle-class welfare, and less to do with the usual culprits of cost of living, population growth and asylum-seeking boatpeople.

Tim Soutphommasane

Elizabeth Farrelly

David Malouf's *The Happy Life* is a creature of many parts, unified more by its gentlemanly prose – as thoughtful and courteous as the man himself – than any driving argument. Notwithstanding its vast discursive arc, through Jefferson and Plato to Rubens, hedonism and the Golden Section, the essay ends pretty much where it begins, with a peasant's-eye view.

Malouf may be right to aver, in his opening line, that happiness is "among the simplest of human emotions." He may be right to end with Solzhenitsyn's Shukhov, a character designed to show us both that happiness is something we make, and that the most reliable sort is small and piecemeal, the kind that, in Malouf's closing words, you "can make do with from one day to the next."

But although this small, personal take on happiness deals fascinatingly and at times brilliantly with the causes of happiness, the essay declines to consider its effects – or, if you will, its costs – which are complex, unforgiving and immense.

It is ironic that happiness should be so much the issue of our time, given that we have more freedom, leisure and wealth than ever. More interesting still is the way happiness has, within a couple of centuries, replaced goodness as the dominant purpose of human life. For this in turn has spawned Happiness as a vast global industry, which, far from ending our voracious pursuit of life satisfaction, spurs it on until the pursuit itself threatens our survival.

At first cut you might think that people have always wanted, in the main, to be happy. You might even argue that other goals (righteousness, say, or enlightenment, or nirvana) are just happiness by another name; that even altruism has selfish ends. But there is a crucial difference between happiness as by-catch and happiness as the main target, and not only because happiness (like God, some might say) is a thing you see only when you're not looking either directly at it or consciously for it.

Malouf offers some valuable insights. I am indebted to him, for instance, for tracing our near-universal sense of entitlement to happiness back to Jefferson's seeding of the American century with the title to "life, liberty and the pursuit of happiness." Malouf rightly notes that this was Jefferson's "real time-bomb," although he never quite gets around to exploring why.

I was also intrigued by Malouf's drawing out of the etymological link between "happiness" and "happenstance." This older usage, taking in external circumstance, puts the traditional idea of "happiness" closer to our notion of "wellbeing" than the more personal, psychological and even spiritual quality we call happiness.

Equally interesting is Malouf's Prometheus–Epimetheus discussion, with its suggestion that human restlessness, which is seen to equate with unhappiness, has always been humanity's main reason for getting out of bed in the morning.

After that, however, I part company with Malouf. Having set this excellent hare running, he refuses to follow it to its lair – namely, whether "happiness" is really desirable, beneficial, achievable or sustainable. Instead, he engages in a soothing discussion of art, beauty and bodily pleasure, without wondering, it seems, whether the leap from pleasure to happiness might need defending. He rightly notes our anxiety at shrinking forests and ice caps but, rather than making the obvious link to our hunger for happiness, drops sideways into a discussion of mind versus brain.

The shift from goodness to happiness remains similarly unremarked, despite its overwhelming consequences.

Where phrases like the "good life" and even the "good death" used to mean morally good, they now just mean pleasurable or, at the very least, without pain. This shrinkage of our goals from large, God-centred virtue to small, self-centred pleasure has both encouraged and fed on modernity's reigning solipsism.

Malouf seems okay with this, reflecting at length on the fact that "the body has always been a source of joy." His last line, about the "kind of happiness he can make do with," confirms the sense of his conclusion, notwithstanding his wistful earlier talk of the "inner life," that a bit of pleasure here and there may be all that we can really hope for.

Here I must disagree. The real task, in my view, is not to obtain pleasure or even happiness, lovely as these are. The real task is to make life – your life – mean something. To make it signify. In this, pleasure and happiness are no more than decoys.

I recognise that this puts me wholly out of step with popular opinion. Whereas the struggle to be "good," as it was once conceived, unavoidably linked the individual with both God (as moral origin) and other beings, happiness, seen so often to inhere in the perfect body or biggest pile, prefers an entirely ego-centric cosmology. This is what makes happiness, and its pursuit, so dangerous.

While even hedonics now recognises the pursuit of goodness as the surest source of the abiding joy that comes from engagement in a greater cause, the pursuit of happiness is its own worst enemy.

Yet just as the fat chick's defence against self-loathing is to eat more chocolate, humanity's balm for guilt about the fate of our planet is to shop more, drink more, get more stuff. Our relentless pursuit of happiness, and our overweening sense of entitlement to it, is taking us all straight over the cliff.

Happiness, in other words, is costing us the earth. That's funny, right?

Elizabeth Farrelly

Gordon Parker

As a psychiatrist, I find that the subject of happiness is never raised directly by my patients. They rightly give priority to seeking relief from psychological pain. My knowledge of the topic is therefore largely derived from the research of psychologists, economists, Buddhists, politicians and science writers. It was a pleasure, then, to read a creative writer's perspective.

David Malouf initially describes happiness as a transient state (what science calls "hedonistic" happiness), although the transience of such states and their lack of sustained impact on health and wellbeing means they are little treated in the academic literature. Others give more weight to "eudemonic happiness," otherwise known as wellbeing, which emphasises a positive outlook, engagement and fulfilment, and is derived from Aristotle's concept of fulfilling one's true nature.

Wellbeing levels appear to be strongly hard-wired: people tend to be either "flourishers" or "languishers" – with corresponding brain activity being greater in either the left or right pre-frontal cortex. This tendency is strongly genetically predisposed and relatively stable. "Set-point theory" argues that everyone has a particular level of wellbeing, with an emotional range of 10–15 per cent around their defined "point." For example, winning the lottery or suffering a major loss will cause a distinct change in short-term happiness or unhappiness, but after a period wellbeing levels will revert to the individual's set point. Such levels link strongly with health and longevity, and they are considered sufficiently important to generate Gross National Happiness measures to complement Gross Domestic Product indices.

Malouf reviews the burdensome lives of our ancestors and notes that it was only very few who had the opportunity, whether through affluence or luck, to cultivate their sense of wellbeing. Our greater privileges and luxuries allow us greater freedoms – especially of retreat and self-contemplation – but Malouf's idea of the aspirant savant in his "little back-shop" is discordant with the empirical findings, which reveal strong and enduring links between wellbeing and socialisation – not with insularity. There are other risks, too, if we give priority to our "garden," seek to be "entirely free" or "wedded only to ourselves" – the risk of self-indulgence, in particular. Solitude's benefits may well be argued for on a short-term basis – as a necessary break from responsibilities and day-to-day pressures – but as an ongoing objective it risks a recoil, such as the anomie described by Milan Kundera in *The Unbearable Lightness of Being*.

Malouf states that the phrase the "good life" no longer raises "the question of how we have lived, of moral qualities." I take issue with this: if we examine Martin Seligman's motivational hierarchy (and Abraham Maslow's hierarchy of needs) for achieving fulfilment, particularly through work, there is a clear moral element. Thus, in Seligman's formulation, Level 1 describes the "pleasant life," where work is simply holding down a job that generates more positive than negative emotions. Level 2 defines the "good life," where the individual uses their positive character strengths for work, love and parenting, and where work is generally viewed as a career. Level 3 defines the "meaningful life," where one's character strengths are used to serve others, and where work provides a "calling." Thus the literature on wellbeing does impute a moral component to the "good life." Aristotle is cogent here: "Happiness is the consequence of a deed." Deed, not need. Thus the phrase the "good life" can currently be applied either without connotations of virtue (as Malouf uses it) or with a distinct sense of fostering strength of character and altruism.

One reason why "happiness" has become such a preoccupation today is that previous generations were encouraged to believe that if disease and pestilence were overcome and labour-saving devices introduced, then we would all be happy. Malouf takes up this enigma. The "Paradox of Happiness" is that, despite such advances having occurred, levels of community wellbeing have remained stable or actually declined – a phenomenon that Randolph Nesse described as "the cruel joke." One reason for this, of course, is the increased materialism that has accompanied such progress.

Malouf perceptively highlights the difficulties in defining "happiness." As noted, some distinguish between hedonistic and eudemonic happiness. How might we discern the latter? First, by examining actual measures of contentment with one's life (but not the smugness of self-satisfaction) – usually by asking people questions like "How satisfied are you with your life as a whole?" and "If you could live your life over, would you wish to substantially change anything?" We might then consider socialisation, social capital, community-mindedness, positivity and openness to experience. One measure, for example, asks the individual to judge whether, in general, they believe that "most people are honest." A seemingly trite question, but it gives a neat signal when you compare such affirmers – who go through life with a Duchenne smile and are open-hearted, giving in spirit, positive about themselves and others – with those who are defensive, misanthropic, pessimistic, negative and inclined more to receive than to give. A link between the two expressions of happiness, hedonism and eudemonia, is that the act of giving to others increases short-term happiness. Happiness as the consequence of a deed – again.

Malouf notes humankind's "restlessness." In essence, a materialistic culture, with its advertising, celebrity style and range of superficial values, leverages that "restlessness" by trying to program us to want everything. However, if we do buy the advertised product, our "happiness" is only temporary – and rapidly sated – as pleasure becomes a matter of course and we then require another "shot." Thus, materialistic people who value money, success, fame and good looks tend to be less satisfied than those who strive for good relationships with others and are active in social causes. "Deed" trumps "need" once more.

Malouf suggests that our current immersion in "multi-tasking" may create a new form of happiness. Unlikely in my view, and worse, it further encourages the individual to continue to pursue happiness – faster and across multiple tasks. The decline in women's levels of wellbeing over the last three decades (men's have largely remained constant) is thought to reflect the increasing pressure on women to fulfil multiple roles (i.e. worker, wife, mother) and to measure their "success" by their capacity to master all tasks. Wellbeing tends to increase when we slow down or "downsize" rather than multi-task and speed up the treadmill to chase happiness.

Malouf's thoughts on the complexion of happiness built into the US Declaration of Independence are fascinating. An additional piece of historical knowledge throws even more light. Jefferson did borrow from the Virginian Constitution's "life and liberty, with the means of acquiring and possessing property, and pursuing and obtaining happiness and safety." But he came to favour the briefer Lockean list of "life, liberty and property." However, Benjamin Franklin then interfered – as was his wont – and is said to have substituted "happiness" for "property." If true, the very act of equating property and acquisition with happiness suggests to me a very early American leaning toward materialism – rather than "optimism," as per Malouf.

Numerous studies – and a Nobel Prize was awarded for economic work in this area – have shown that individuals earning large amounts of money are not much happier than those on low incomes (grinding poverty excepted). Why do children in ghettos often display happiness despite their deprivation? Essentially, if we "fit" within our group, we are not necessarily unhappy. It is only when we compare ourselves with others in our group or society and feel that we are "falling behind" that our happiness is compromised. The "relative consumption" theory is all-important here – what generates unhappiness is not having too little but being disconcerted by having less than others. Thus, the messages from wellbeing studies are that:

(i) happiness does not equate with materialistic success;
(ii) you can't successfully chase happiness; and
(iii) if you wish to increase your levels of wellbeing, you should slow down and respect a set of ethical principles.

Wellbeing does not correlate strongly with the factors Malouf suggests statisticians use to gauge societal happiness: equality of opportunity, justice, civil liberty, employment, food and housing. Rather, it is strongly linked to relationships, marriage and family, efficacy (i.e. enjoyable life goals effectively managed), finding a "meaning" in life (be it a religion, spirituality or a secular philosophy), fulfilment in work and (to some degree) good health. We increase our level of wellbeing by such things and by challenging ourselves – the challenge is best when it is valued, self-generated and neither too hard nor too easy – and by "optimisation" (finding positive meanings in ordinary events or even in adversity itself).

The central tenets of the academic literature are that happiness:

(i) requires reciprocity with others;
(ii) is achieved more by seeking purpose and meaning in life than from material gain; and
(iii) comes from within and from relationships rather than from externally judged "success."

I was therefore somewhat perplexed by Malouf's assessment of Solzhenitsyn's Shukhov – an inmate of a Soviet gulag serving a term of 3653 days, who had eaten an extra bowl of porridge for dinner, cut a good deal with a gang leader, enjoyed building a wall, evaded being caught in a search and bought some tobacco. Malouf states that "Shukhov is our *perfect example of the happy man*," but Solzhenitsyn merely describes his protagonist Shukhov's one day as "*almost* happy," as he has had "many strokes of luck that day." Shukhov is indeed satisfied that he has made the day "work" for him, but is he the quintessential happy chappy? There is a rather Calvinistic flavour to Malouf's view – that to experience happiness, we must know pain – and perhaps the implication here is that more pain leads to greater happiness. Myself, I think Shukhov would have known happiness if the warden of the gulag had unlocked his cell that night and said, "Sorry, comrade. Stalin's just telegrammed an apology. It was all a mistake – you're free to go." Then I could imagine Shukhov as a happy man – but only briefly. Winning such a lottery would generate only ephemeral euphoria before "set-point theory" became operative and a free Shukhov reverted to being a lugubrious languisher – the Russian states being consistently identified as having the lowest levels of community happiness. But perhaps I'm being too negative.

Gordon Parker

Judith Brett is one of Australia's leading political commentators and the author of two previous *Quarterly Essays*, *Exit Right* and *Relaxed and Comfortable*. Her books include the award-winning *Robert Menzies' Forgotten People*, *Ordinary People's Politics* (with Anthony Moran) and *Australian Liberals and the Moral Middle Class: From Alfred Deakin to John Howard*. She is professor of politics at La Trobe University.

Robert Dessaix is a writer, translator, broadcaster and essayist. His books include *A Mother's Disgrace*, *Corfu* and the travel memoirs *Twilight of Love: Travels with Turgenev* and, most recently, *Arabesques: A Tale of Double Lives*.

Elizabeth Farrelly is a columnist for the *Sydney Morning Herald* and the author of *Blubberland: The Dangers of Happiness*.

Robert Lagerberg is a senior lecturer in Russian at the University of Melbourne.

Anne Manne is the author of *Motherhood: How Should We Care for Our Children?*, short-listed for the Walkley non-fiction prize, and *So This Is Life: Tales from a Country Childhood*.

Gordon Parker is Scientia Professor of Psychiatry at the University of New South Wales and Executive Director of the Black Dog Institute. In 2007 he took part in a Sydney debate on happiness with the Dalai Lama.

Tim Soutphommasane is a political philosopher and the author of *Reclaiming Patriotism* and the Per Capita report *What Crisis? Wellbeing and the Australian Quality of Life*. A research fellow at Monash University's National Centre for Australian Studies, he writes the "Ask the Philosopher" column for the *Weekend Australian*.

www.ingramcontent.com/pod-product-compliance
Lightning Source LLC
Chambersburg PA
CBHW061237270326
41930CB00024B/3499